Margaret Sanger

Rebel for Women's Rights

Women in Medicine

Karen Horney
Pioneer of Feminine Psychology

Mathilde Krim and the Story of AIDS

Elisabeth Kübler-Ross
Encountering Death and Dying

Rita Levi-Montalcini
Nobel Prize Winner

Mary Eliza Mahoney
and the Legacy of African-American Nurses

Margaret Sanger
Rebel for Women's Rights

WOMEN in MEDICINE

Margaret Sanger

Rebel for Women's Rights

Vicki Cox

CHELSEA HOUSE
PUBLISHERS

A Haights Cross Communications Company

Philadelphia

COVER: Margaret Sanger preparing to defend her case before the federal government in New York. Her book *The Woman Rebel* broke the Comstock law, which prohibited the transport by public mail of any literature regarding contraception.

CHELSEA HOUSE PUBLISHERS
VP, NEW PRODUCT DEVELOPMENT Sally Cheney
DIRECTOR OF PRODUCTION Kim Shinners
CREATIVE MANAGER Takeshi Takahashi
MANUFACTURING MANAGER Diann Grasse

Staff for MARGARET SANGER
EXECUTIVE EDITOR Lee M. Marcott
PHOTO EDITOR Sarah Bloom
PRODUCTION EDITOR Noelle Nardone
SERIES & COVER DESIGNER Takeshi Takahashi
LAYOUT 21st Century Publishing and Communications, Inc.

A Haights Cross Communications ✧ Company

http://www.chelseahouse.com

First Printing

9 8 7 6 5 4 3 2 1

Library of Congress Cataloging-in-Publication Data

Cox, Vicki.
  Margaret Sanger / Vicki Cox.
    p. cm.—(Women in medicine)
  ISBN 0-7910-8030-7
  1. Sanger, Margaret, 1879–1966. 2. Birth control—United States—
Biography. 3. Women social reformers—United States—Biography.
I. Title. II. Series.
HQ764.S3C68 2004
363.9'6'092—dc22
                                                    2004006048

All links and web addresses were checked and verified to be correct at the time of publication. Because of the dynamic nature of the web, some addresses and links may have changed since publication and may no longer be valid.

Table of Contents

The Rebel
Goes to Jail

1

"You, Margaret Sanger, are under arrest,"[1] said a New York City policewoman as she entered Margaret Sanger's clinic in the Brownsville section of Brooklyn, New York. Like the Biblical Goliath, Mrs. Whitehurst, a large, thick-bodied woman strode into its unassuming offices to take custody of the petite, soft-spoken Margaret Sanger. The first birth control clinic in America hardly looked like a crime scene. Whitehurst's declaration broke the white tranquility of two freshly painted rooms. In the clinic's outer office, a young woman quietly read to the women who waited to talk to Sanger about the "secret" of preventing pregnancies. The pamphlet the women heard was Sanger's own, "What Every Girl Should Know." Babies lay or sat in their mother's laps. Toddlers played near them.

Whitehurst and the three members of the vice squad who followed her terrified the waiting women. Some started crying. One woman screamed. The babies and toddlers started wailing.

Vice squad members locked the clinic's door, and another policeman stood guard. They seized the medical records of 464 patients who had visited Sanger. They hustled the medical examining table, boxes of contraceptive devices, pamphlets, and furniture into the waiting police van. They made the women in the waiting room line up and forced them to give their names and addresses as if they were criminals.

Actually, only three women had broken the law. Thirty-seven-year-old Margaret Sanger and her sister, Ethel Byrne, had quite purposefully and openly committed the crime of teaching women about their own bodies and explaining ways they could prevent pregnancies. Fania Mindell, their young volunteer assistant, was accused of selling "indecent" literature, Sanger's small pamphlet about the female reproductive system and contraception.[2]

The confusion and chaos the police caused on that October afternoon in 1916 was exactly what Margaret Sanger wanted to have happen. She wanted a crowd outside her clinic. She wanted the newspaper reporters and photographers there, too. She wanted to be arrested. She wanted to go to court. Most of all, she wanted to challenge the laws that decreed only physicians could tell women about **contraception**, the intentional prevention of pregnancy, and only if it was to prevent or cure diseases.

Sanger later said, "I wanted the interpretation to be broad enough to protect women from ill health as the result of excessive child bearing and [for them] to have the right to control their own destinies."[3]

Despite her cool calculations, Sanger's Irish temper flared when she came face to face with Whitehurst. Later she would describe herself as "white hot with indignation."[4]

She shouted at Mrs. Whitehurst, "You dirty thing. You are not a woman. You are a dog."

"Tell that to the judge in the morning," Whitehurst responded.

"No, I'll tell it to you now," Sanger shouted back. "You dog, and you have two ears to hear me, too."[5]

Away from the clinic, Margaret Sanger didn't look or act like a controversial person. Yet even before she opened the Brownsville Clinic, the mere mention of her name inspired either strong admiration or livid hatred. No one was lukewarm about her or her mission: to educate desperate women in preventing or planning pregnancies.

The **Comstock Law**, a federal statute that criminalized **contraceptives**—any device, drug, or chemical agent that prevents conception—had been on the books since 1873. This law made it a federal offense to disseminate birth control information through the mail or across state lines. State laws enacted their own versions of Comstock laws that further restricted the sale of contraceptives. Margaret Sanger and others made it their mission to change these laws. As a visiting nurse in the crowded New York slums, Sanger had been asked many times how to limit pregnancies. She discovered that the only thing women did know how to do was get an abortion. Those who couldn't afford the $5 fee at a back-alley type of clinic often tried to end their pregnancies themselves using knitting needles, umbrella tips, or shoe hooks. Sanger saw first-hand the tragic results of these attempts.

People in some European countries held more enlight-ened views of birth control, encouraging contraceptive use and limiting family size. In Holland, the government supported birth control clinics. Having visited and studied these Dutch clinics, Sanger modeled the Brownsville Clinic after them. But no American institution supported Sanger in her efforts to open her clinic. The New York County Medical Society called selling contraceptive products "absurd, frequently dangerous, filthy and usually unsatisfactory." It said that they would under-mine "personal morality and national strength."[6] Churches vehemently opposed birth control. In particular, the Roman Catholic Church believed that since children were sent by God, any "unnatural" device or practice that prevented their arrival was interfering with His holy will. Some people felt that contraceptive devices promoted casual sexual behavior. Some believed that women should keep having babies to make sure there was enough workers for the work force. Others thought having large families was a patriotic thing for women to do to keep the nation's population high.

Among the poor in particular, women often got pregnant immediately after giving birth to a baby. These babies were born into families with scarce food and little money to buy it. Multiple pregnancies exhausted, and sometimes killed, the mothers. Sanger's own mother was pregnant 18 times in 22 years. She died at the age of 45.

At first, Sanger hunted for a physician to work in the birth control clinic. But no doctors stepped forward, fearing their private practices and their licenses might be affected. So Sanger and her sister decided to open the clinic on their own. Being practical and registered nurses, they felt qualified to talk to women about their reproductive organs and tell them about devices that could prevent pregnancy.

Sanger made sure her plan for a birth control clinic was well known. She kept the newspapers informed of her intentions. In July 1916, months before the clinic opened, she publicized the general area where the clinic would be and when it would open. A *New York Times* article reported that trained nurses, not doctors, would dispense information. Such an obvious violation of the law practically dared the authorities to take action.

Searching for a clinic location, Sanger was turned away by individual landlords and social agencies who said, "We don't want any trouble. Keep out of this district."[7] She scoured neighborhoods for rooms to rent, eventually finding two rooms at 46 Amboy Street. In one of the most congested sections of Brooklyn, the small building was jammed between apartment buildings. Laundry flapped out the windows above the storefront. The sidewalks and street were crowded with vendors and wagons.

A $50 donation by a California supporter paid the first month's rent. Sanger's friends donated a coal stove, blackboard, examining table, furniture, and supplies.

To drum up clients for the clinic, Sanger printed 5,000 pamphlets in English, Yiddish (a language spoken by many Jews) and Italian. They read:

"Mothers! Can you afford to have a large family?

Do you want any more children?

If not, why do you have them?

Do not kill, do not take life, but prevent.

Safe, harmless information can be obtained of trained nurses. Tell your friends and neighbors. All mothers welcome"[8]

Sanger, Byrne, and Mindell slipped the advertisements under doorways and gave them to women on the streets.

Sanger wrote Brooklyn's District Attorney to make sure the authorities knew of her plans. She alerted druggists to increase their stock of devices that could be legally bought, such as pessaries. **Pessaries**, rings that are inserted into the vagina, helped mothers whose multiple pregnancies had weakened the muscles around the uterus. Unofficially, they were believed to prevent **conception**, the fertilization of an egg by a sperm.

Two weeks before the Brownsville Clinic actually opened, she told a *New York Times* reporter about her birth control clinic. She announced she had found a location for the clinic, but would not reveal the address. In the article, the reporter also dutifully reminded his readers that "New York law forbids the dissemination of knowledge on the subject."[9] By this time, the elements of a good drama were in place.

An hour before Sanger opened the doors on October 16, women had already lined up halfway down the street. They came pushing their baby carriages and leading their toddlers. They came alone, with female friends, and with their husbands. Fania Mindell carefully recorded the number of pregnancies, number of children, and number of children's deaths of each woman. She also read Sanger's pamphlet to the women while they waited.

In the examining room, Sanger and Byrne talked to the women in groups of eight. Using diagrams, models, and drawings, they taught women how their bodies worked. They told them about female contraceptive devices. The two nurses sometimes fitted women with diaphragms or gave them pessaries. They told them the names and addresses of pharmacists who might sell them contraceptive equipment.

Sanger and Byrne talked to 140 women the first day. The total surged to 464 during the week and a half the clinic was open. Women came from as far away as Connecticut, Massachusetts, and New Jersey for Sanger's advice. They told her their hopeless circumstances. One woman said her priest had told her to bear many children.

"I had fifteen. Six are living," she said. "I'm thirty-seven years old now. Look at me! I might be fifty."[10]

The neighborhood quickly accepted the clinic. A German bakery sent donuts. The landlord's wife, who lived above the clinic, brewed tea for Sanger and her colleagues. Two policemen making their rounds stopped at the clinic to talk about the weather. The postman who delivered the stacks of letters that Sanger received each day left saying, "Farewell, ladies; hope I find you here tomorrow."[11]

On the ninth day, an unusual woman came into the clinic, repeating a sad story about too many children and not enough money. But she was too well fed, dressed too elegantly, and sounded too educated to have lived among the poor. On her way out, she paid $2 for a copy of Sanger's 10¢ pamphlet. She was so obviously a police undercover agent that Mindell took her money and pinned it to the wall along with a note, "Received from Mrs.————of the Police Department as her contribution."[12]

The moment Sanger had been anticipating came the next day, October 26, when Policewoman Whitehurst strode into the clinic, brandishing all her authority. Sanger's opportunity to challenge the Comstock laws had arrived. Still, Sanger's arrest did not play out quietly. She was angered by the way the police ransacked the clinic, taking confidential medical records. She was outraged by the way the authorities treated her patients. She talked for 30 minutes, calming the hysterical women and persuading the police to release them. A male officer, Sergeant David J. Barry said, "Mrs. Sanger, put on your hat and coat and come quietly with us to the station house."

"I don't know about that," she replied. "I think if you want to take me to your old station house, you'll have to drag me there."[13]

She and Mindell were "half dragged" and "half carried"[14] towards the patrol wagon and away from the newspaper photographers and supporters who had gathered outside. But the police could not make her get into the patrol wagon.

Instead, she insisted on marching the mile to the Raymond Street jail. It was quite a spectacle. Sanger and Mindell, accompanied by the policemen, were followed by the women who had been at the clinic and the crowd that had gathered. One woman, who had just arrived at the clinic, deserted her baby carriage and ran after Sanger and Mindell yelling, "Come back! Come back and save me."[15]

Sanger was charged with breaking Section 1142 of the New York State Penal Code, which forbade anyone to "sell, lend, or give away," or to "advertise, loan, or distribute 'any recipe, drug or medicine for the prevention of conception.'"[16] Byrne, who had been away from the clinic but arrested later, was charged under the same Section. Mindell was charged with selling obscene literature.

The women could have posted their $500 bail and left. Instead, they chose to generate more publicity by spending the night in the company of the jail's cockroaches and rats. Margaret Sanger's public fight for the woman's right to determine the number and spacing of her pregnancies hit newspapers throughout the country. The delicate champion for birth control had thrown the first stone at the law.

The Rebel
Prepares

2

At the end of the 19th century, Corning, New York, was a factory town with two classes. Poor workers lived down the hill beside the Chemung River. Factory owners and the rich lived in the hills, away from the pollution of the smokestacks. The Irish-Catholic Higgins family lived in a shack on the river flats. The railroad tracks ran just outside the front door.

Margaret Louisa Higgins was born on September 14, 1879. As an adult, Margaret Sanger lied about her age. She tried to change her birth date to that of her younger sister's in the family Bible. Later, when the ink faded, her mother's inscription told the truth.

Margaret's mother, Anne, was a model of everything Margaret later came to hate. The slender, black-haired, green-eyed beauty spent her days cooking, cleaning, and washing for her husband and 11 children. She loved her husband and rarely argued with him. While her husband blustered about politics, she carried in the firewood. She put wild flowers on the table and rinsed her daughters' red hair in rainwater to make it shine. However, she was sick with **tuberculosis**, at the time a deadly disease that was made worse by many pregnancies. Her tubercular cough was so strong that she had to lean against a wall to recover.

Margaret's father, Michael Higgins, was the model for her life's work. Her social awareness came from her father, calling his radicalism "the spring"[17] from which she drank. He ignored the status quo. When style dictated short hair, mustache, and beard, he wore his red hair long and shaved his face. Higgins argued long and loud about social justice and reform, seemingly more concerned that factory workers earned $2.00 for a 10-hour day than with supporting his own family. He was a stonemason whose job depended on carving gravestones out of marble. He lost his best customer, the Catholic Church, because he criticized organized religion and invited atheists and reformers to speak in Corning.

Like her father, Margaret would later support labor unions. She would walk picket lines and get arrested. Like her father, she constantly fought the Catholic Church, only her cause was birth control.

Michael Higgins loved his own children, but other priorities came first. Higgins took money meant to buy the family's winter coal supply to bankroll a dinner/lecture to impress the town's leading citizens. Sent to get a few bananas for his children, he bought an entire stalk and gave it away on the way home. His sons wore their sisters' clothes while Anne mended their pants, yet vagrants, stopping by the Higgins home, were always fed.

Called Maggie as a child, Margaret Higgins had a small frame, with fine features and her mother's wide-set eyes. The sixth child of 11, she quickly learned adult skills like bathing or rocking her baby brothers to sleep for her mother. Her father drew Margaret into his unorthodox activities. In 1882, she stood guard while he unearthed the casket of 4-year-old, Henry, who had died of pneumonia. He opened his son's coffin and made a plaster of Paris death mask of the boy for his grieving wife.

Two years later, he took Margaret with him to hear atheist Richard Ingersoll speak. The priest ordered the doors of the town hall locked, and Margaret along with other Ingersoll supporters were pelted with tomatoes thrown by the Christian crowd. Michael Higgins's politics branded his children. After the Ingersoll riot, their classmates called them "children of the devil."[18]

Margaret accepted the name calling, but her Irish temper exploded when her 8th-grade teacher ridiculed her for looking at her birthday present in class. Her teacher said, "Miss Higgins, you are so busy admiring your gloves, you seem to be above a little thing like paying attention."[19] The class laughed. Maggie ran home, declaring she would not return. "I'll go to jail! I'll work, I'll starve, I'll die, but back to that school and teacher I will never go."[20] Her parents and family could not persuade her to finish the last two weeks of the term.

In 1896, her parents enrolled her in Claverack College and Hudson River Institute, about three miles from Hudson, New York. To pay for her tuition, two of her sisters worked as housekeepers. Margaret worked in the school's dining room. In this larger world of 500 students, little Maggie blossomed into Margaret Higgins. Seventeen-year-old Margaret was a fun-loving beauty. She wore her auburn hair in braids. High-necked blouses tapered into tight-waisted long skirts that flattered her slender figure. She loved to dance and act in plays. Her high spirits and laughter attracted many friends. Posing for school photos, she couldn't resist flirting with the camera.

"She was one of the most popular girls in school," recalled Amelia Stuart, a close friend. "She attracted confidences without ever asking for them."[21]

Like her father, Margaret loved to debate, especially controversial issues. She backed unpopular William Jennings Bryan in the 1896 presidential election. Her first speech was on women's rights. Some boys thought the topic hilarious and drew cartoons of Margaret in pants and smoking a cigar.

The woman who later would address thousands feared speaking in public. "I studied. . . stealing away to the cemetery and standing on the monuments over the graves," she said. "Each day in the quiet of the dead, I repeated and repeated that speech out loud."[22]

Though dating was forbidden, Claverack boys and girls often met secretly. Margaret and her friends once sneaked out a window to meet boys at a local dance hall. Discovered by the principal, they were marched back to school. Margaret was lectured on using her leadership abilities properly.

Unable to finance her last year at Claverack, Margaret applied at a New York acting school. But the application wanted ankle, calf, knee, thigh, breast, and hip measurements. "But to see such personal information go coldly down on paper to be sent off to strange men was unthinkable,"[23] she wrote.

Tuberculosis

Tuberculosis, or consumption, is a contagious disease that has been found in 4,000-year-old Egyptian mummies. The bacteria that cause the disease, *Mycobacterium tuberculosis,* are transmitted from person to person through microscopic droplets expelled into the air by coughing or sneezing. Tuberculosis can settle in any part of the body, but usually attacks the lungs. Its symptoms include cough and sputum (coughed up mucus), fatigue, loss of appetite, loss of weight, fever, night sweats, and coughing up blood.

Around 1854, just twenty years before Margaret Sanger was born, the first effective treatment of the disease was discovered. Doctors found that fresh air improved the patient's health. They began isolating patients in places called sanatoriums, where they were treated with a routine of fresh air, complete bed rest, and a nutritional diet. The sanatoriums also served to isolate sick individuals from the healthy population.

Because tuberculosis bacteria thrive on oxygen, doctors later treated tuberculosis by collapsing the infected lung. With less oxygen, the disease did not spread so fast. Another treatment involved surgically removing the hard nodules that form when tuberculosis attacks other parts of the body. It was only in 1943 that an effective antibiotic—streptomycin—was found to treat it. With the development of this and other antibiotics, the incidence of tuberculosis in industrialized countries declined even more rapidly. In the past two decades, however, the incidence of tuberculosis in the United States has increased. This is due to immigration of individuals from developing countries, where the incidence of tuberculosis is still high, and also to the human immuno-deficiency virus (HIV). Because HIV-infected people have weakened immune systems, they have a much greater chance of developing tuberculosis.

Thoughts about acting disappeared, and Margaret found a job teaching 84 immigrant 1st graders who spoke no English. She lasted six months, until her mother's tuberculosis worsened, and Margaret came home to nurse her.

"Although she was now spitting up blood when she coughed," Margaret later recalled, "we still expected her to live on forever."[24] Fifty-year-old Anne Higgins died on March 31, 1899, worn out by her many pregnancies, her demanding life, and tuberculosis. Margaret was expected to take over washing, ironing, cooking, mending, and tending her younger sister and brothers.

Her father's grief for the woman he truly loved turned him into an "irritable, aggravating tyrant."[25] He ruled Margaret and her younger sister Ethel with an iron fist. "Whatever we did was wrong," she recalled. "He objected particularly to young men."[26] He set a strict 10 P.M. curfew. Once when his daughters arrived home late, he pulled Ethel inside the house and locked Margaret out. For the pretty young woman who had dated several boys at Claverack and even discussed marriage with one of them, the situation was oppressive. Margaret wanted out.

After reading medical books on tuberculosis as she tended her mother, Margaret longed to be a physician. Lacking the funds for medical school, she turned to nursing. In 1900, a year after her mother died, Margaret headed to White Plains Hospital, just outside of New York City. Conditions in the 12-bed hospital were primitive. The three-story structure had no electricity, heat, or plumbing. There was just one bathroom on each floor. As a probationary nurse, she enrolled in a two-year training program that "tested character, integrity, nerve, patience and endurance."[27]

Margaret admitted patients, wrote case histories, and trudged up and down stairs to dispense drinking water and empty bedpans. She boiled linens, changed bandages, and observed surgeries. With no doctor on call, Margaret and the dozen probationary nurses handled patient care. This was often not an easy task. A deranged patient once attacked her with a knife; another knocked her into a wall.

For at-home deliveries, she arrived before the doctor to sterilize the instruments. If the doctor was late, she delivered the baby herself. The mothers confided feelings they couldn't tell a male doctor. One said, "I have had four babies and three miscarriages in the past ten years. I don't have the strength for another pregnancy."[28] Another, desperate to prevent another pregnancy, asked, "Miss Higgins, what should I do not to have another baby right away?"[29]

Margaret, who knew nothing about contraception, would tell the doctor. Margaret later wrote, "The doctor, more often than not, snorted, 'She ought to be ashamed of herself to talk to a young girl about things like that.'"[30]

The demanding work sapped her energy. Margaret developed tuberculosis, probably caught from her mother. After an operation to contain it, she missed several weeks of school. To begin her third year, she transferred to New York City's Manhattan Eye and Ear Infirmary to make up credits she lost during her illness.

There, Margaret Higgins met William Sanger at a hospital dance when the 28-year-old architect delivered blueprints to Margaret's supervisor. The men invited Margaret to look over the plans. A "sudden electric quality"[31] passed between Bill and Margaret. Bill Sanger was absolutely smitten. He waited all night to walk her home after her shift ended. He sent her flowers, jewelry, and a gold watch. He called and wrote her every day. Margaret found Bill romantic, intense, and idealistic. Like her father, he talked loudly about economic reform and social justice and rejected conventional religion.

As six months passed, she agreed to marry Bill, but she wanted to postpone the marriage until she graduated and could pay for the wedding. She jokingly wrote her sisters that a "good way to save expense would be to have him [William] on the verge of death, and I can nurse him & insist on a deathbed marriage."[32]

For Bill, getting married was a "now or never" proposition. He was afraid some doctor might sweep her off her feet. On August 18, 1902, Bill took Margaret for a carriage ride between her nursing shifts. Their conversation turned to marriage. Since nursing students could not be married, Margaret wanted to wait. Bill was prepared to marry right then. He brought the marriage license with him and had arranged for a minister to perform the ceremony. Overwhelmed, Margaret Higgins married William Sanger in an old blue work dress and returned in time for her shift.

Margaret had conflicting emotions about her hastily arranged wedding. She told her sisters, "I vow I will not live with such a beast of a man," but shortly afterward exclaimed, "I am sure I could not have a better husband."[33] Whichever way Margaret really felt, her nursing studies were over. She was forced to resign. Her husband underestimated this bitter sacrifice to their sweet love. He later wrote, "I didn't realize it would loom in such prodigious proportions."[34]

Bill Sanger's Socialist leanings did not extend to his marriage. He wanted Margaret to be a housewife and nothing else. For her to work outside the home would be unthinkable. Two weeks after their wedding, they were living in a Manhattan apartment. Like a good wife, she was pregnant within six months. Unfortunately, her tuberculosis returned along with the pregnancy.

She went to a **sanatorium**, a hospital where people were treated for diseases like tuberculosis, in New York's Adirondack Mountains. Prescribed treatments included bed rest, large quantities of food, and clean air. Wrapped in thick blankets, Margaret spent hours outside. The thin air of high altitudes supposedly kept germs from the oxygen that fed them. She ate a daily diet of a dozen eggs, four quarts of milk, meat, and vegetables. She swallowed capsules of creosote, a toxin made from wood tar that was thought to be effective against infection.

She returned to New York City for the birth of her baby. On November 28, 1903, she delivered Stuart, named for her friend Amelia Stuart. Then Margaret went back to the sanitarium, staying at a nearby farmhouse with Stuart. For eight months, Margaret's condition did not improve. She became increasingly depressed and indifferent to her baby. Finally a doctor got through to her, saying, "Do something. Want something."[35] Margaret realized that she wanted one thing: to go home. She packed up Stuart, his nurse, and sent Bill a telegram to meet them at the train station. Away from the sanatorium's focus on invalidism, she recovered.

Searching for a place to live away from the polluted city, the Sangers found Columbia Colony in the town of Hastings-on-Hudson, a community of young, professional, and artistic people. Margaret once again settled into homemaking and motherhood. She took her turn teaching in the community's kindergarten. She found Hastings-on-Hudson existence quiet to the point of "spiritual stagnation."[36]

Bill threw himself into planning and constructing a "showplace."[37] The white stucco house included a studio for Bill to paint, a dining room, library, nursery with veranda, bathrooms in all the bedrooms, and fireplaces everywhere. Margaret and Bill stained the woodwork themselves. Bill, skilled in stained glassmaking, designed a magnificent rose window; husband and wife assembled it together. The Sangers moved into their house February 1908. One evening Bill built a large fire in the furnace. That night their maid woke them crying, "Madam! Come! Fire in the big stove."[38] Margaret, now pregnant, ran to the nursery for Stuart, and Bill went for help. With flames threatening their escape route, Margaret covered the toddler's head and hurried down the stairs. The fire demolished their beautiful rose window and nearly everything else.

Salvaging what they could, they rebuilt the house and lived in it for three years. But Margaret complained it smelled of smoke and burned wood. Five months after the fire, in July 1908, Grant Sanger was born. Peggy (named after Margaret) followed in 1910.

While Margaret loved her children, she also neglected them to the point that "thrifty, good housekeeping neighbors took them into their laps, removed the safety pins that held their clothes together and sewed on a proper button."[39]

One day, in 1910, Margaret overheard a foreman criticizing his crew for their indifference to the labor struggle. The foreman, a Socialist, seeing Margaret's interest, gave her clippings of the Socialist newspaper, *The New York Call.* That moment transformed her. Her husband later wrote, "She devoured every article and book she could lay her capable hands on. . . . She got to know the leaders of the Social and radical labor movements. . . . Gone forever was the conservative Irish girl I had married; a new woman, forceful, intelligent, hungry for facts, tireless, ambitious and cool, had miraculously come into being."[40]

The $12,000 debt of building a home two times overwhelmed the Sangers. They sold the property and moved into an apartment in New York City. Bill's mother moved in to care for the children (now aged 8, 3, and 1) so that Margaret could earn extra money as a visiting nurse. It was Margaret's escape from the domestic life she detested and the door to her destiny.

The Rebel
Awakens

3

The Sangers' move to New York City transported Margaret Sanger into two totally different worlds: the politics of reform and the despair of poverty.

The rebels, "politicians, painters, sociologists, sexologists, futurists, dramatists, sculptors, editors, writers, anarchists, and poets," already knew Bill.[41] They included the Sangers in their discussions about America's flawed society. When they gathered together, the Sangers sat beside the blue-ribbon list of America's critics. Will Durant, a philosopher and writer, lectured on the sex psychology of Havelock Ellis, a man who would later influence Margaret Sanger's public and private life. John Reed, a journalist and intellectual, described the Mexican Revolution. Walter Lippmann, a writer and political commentator, talked about psychiatrist Sigmund Freud. They knew the playwright Eugene O'Neill, the writer Upton Sinclair, and the anarchist Emma Goldman, who had loudly crusaded for "voluntary motherhood" for ten years. They met Eugene V. Debs, the leader of the American **Socialist party**, a political party that sought to organize society in a way that served for the benefit of all, rather than for the profit of a few. Many left-wing leaders came to the Sanger apartment. While Margaret served cocoa and listened, they argued if there should be a government at all, how it should be changed, whether the government should control business, and how to eliminate social injustice.

The Sangers joined the New York Socialist Party Local No. 5 in Harlem. Bill ran as a municipal alderman on the Socialist ticket but lost. Margaret became an "organizer" for the woman's committee and was paid $15 a week to recruit new members among Irish women in the laundry union and Scandinavians in the housemaid union. She handed out pamphlets and spoke on street corners.

With Bill's mother babysitting the children, the Sangers attended many meetings. Grant wished his mother would stay home. Climbing into her lap one evening, he told her, "Oh,

I hate soshism [his word for Socialism]!"[42] Margaret went to the meeting anyway.

She was still very quiet at the gatherings, absorbing everyone's comments. She would whisper her ideas into Bill's ear, and he would tell the others, "Margaret has something to say on that. Have you heard Margaret?"[43]

Sanger kept listening. She enrolled Stuart in a school where people described as free thinkers taught. She attended their lectures at night, taking in everything. She read the Socialist newspaper, *The New York Call.* She also read *The Masses*, a

Socialism

Socialism was a political movement that began in the 1800s. It sprang up because of the terrible working conditions that developed from the Industrial Revolution in Europe, and later, in the United States.

Socialists wanted to improve the lives of people who worked long hours for very little pay. They wanted to eliminate their suffering and help them have a better way of life.

Instead of individuals owning factories and the country's resources, Socialists wanted the government to be in charge. Socialists believed the government could solve social problems like poverty and conflicts between factory owners and its workers. They believed everyone could be treated equally and fairly.

In the United States, the movement grew under the leadership of Eugene V. Debs. In 1912, dues-paying Socialists numbered 118,000 members. Debs received almost a million votes in 1912 and 1920 presidential elections. The popularity of Socialism may have declined because of World War I. Instead of criticizing the government, people wanted to be patriotic and support it. Another reason may have been that Socialism was just too far away from the rights of the individual that are found in the United States Constitution.

publication that viewed the Catholic Church as a major obstacle to progress. Margaret would come to that conclusion herself in six short years.

Associating with those with radical political views destroyed Bill's architectural career. He turned to painting, a pursuit that did not support his growing household that now included Bill's mother and Margaret's sister, Ethel Byrne. She left her husband and children to become a nurse. After she finished her degree, Ethel returned home to get her children back. But her in-laws went to court, and she lost custody of her children. Bill and Margaret helped with her legal expenses. They kept in touch with her children. Ethel's daughter, Olive, remembered Margaret's affection. "I always thought of her as Christmas," she said. "She had red hair and sparkling green eyes, and she opened her arms to me and hugged me."[44] In return, Ethel helped get Margaret nursing jobs at the Visiting Nurse's Association. As a part-time visiting nurse, Margaret took cases on the Lower East Side of New York City. There, Irish, Jewish, Italian, and German immigrants were jammed 3,000 people to the square block in places with colorful names like "Hell's Kitchen," "New Israel," and "Little Italy."

Sanger was shocked by the conditions she saw in the rundown apartment houses, called **tenements**. There, "below Fourteenth Street," she wrote, "I seemed to be breathing a different air, to be in another world and country."[45] In this world of the hopeless poor, men, women, and children worked 14-hour days. People slept six to a room. Three floors in a tenement shared one bathroom. Women dragged garbage down flights of stairs and dumped it on the streets, where their children played. Women were always pregnant and seemingly ignorant about how their bodies functioned.

Sanger wrote, "Ignorance and neglect go on day by day, children born to breathe but a few hours and pass out of life, pregnant women toiling early and late to give food to four or five children, always hungry, boarders taken into homes where there is not sufficient room for the family. "[46] Sanger hoped that the Socialist Party would correct conditions in the tenements. It distributed millions of pamphlets to working women—homemakers, garment factory workers, department store salesgirls, and teachers. The Party supported women's right to vote, although not very enthusiastically. She liked the idea of a society where everyone shared things equally. After three years of listening and studying, Sanger didn't whisper any more. The horrible conditions she saw were reasons enough to speak out. By 1911, she was writing articles for *The New York Call.* Her radical friends' vocabulary had become her own.

From March to December 1911, Sanger wrote articles blasting the inequalities between wealthy women and tenement women. She described the terrible conditions in the tenements. She urged working women to join the Socialist Party and "pull down completely this system which mangles and stunts the minds, morals, and bodies of our boys and women. . . to crush and stamp it out forever."[47]

Anita Block, one of *The Call's* editors, asked Sanger to fill in for a speaker at a Socialist meeting. Though still shy about public speaking, she agreed. Instead of talking about labor issues, Sanger lectured on health, something she knew more about. The second time she talked, her 10-person audience had grown to 75. She continued her lectures, describing the terrible conditions she saw in the tenements and venting her frustration that no one would educate women about their own bodies. Block then asked Sanger to write a series for *The Call's* women's pages. "How Six Little Children Were Told the Truth" was based on talks about reproduction she had with her son Stuart and his friends at Hastings-on-Hudson. The series was groundbreaking journalism for a time when sex was never mentioned in public by men, let alone by a woman.

Block introduced the series by explaining that Sanger wrote the stories from "actual experience" rather than theory.[48]

The series included stories about plants, toads, birds, and mammals, describing matter-of-factly the process of fertilization in each species. She told her readers that "The one unpardonable sin on the part of a mother is to let her children learn the truth elsewhere than from her lips." [49]

Ironically, even as Sanger wrote for the Socialist Party, she realized that the slow process of change through negotiations, compromise, and the ballot box would not affect the poor women she saw. The talk in the Party always skirted away from women's needs toward improving men's workplaces. She left the party on January 25, 1912, and drifted towards "direct action" organizations, like labor unions, that used confrontation to achieve their goals.

Sanger didn't have to wait long to step into the action. The mill workers in Lawrence, Massachusetts, making $6 or $7 a week, refused their owners' proposed pay cut. They went on strike, declaring, "Better to starve fighting than to starve working!" [50]

Backed by the **Industrial Workers of the World (IWW)**, a radical labor organization, the strike affected over 22,000 workers, stopping virtually all production at the mills. In a fight between strikers and policemen, a woman picketer was killed. After picketing through January and February, the strikers were out of money. In the bitter New England winter, their children went hungry. Both to help the children and to gain publicity for the strikers, the IWW strike committee asked Sanger and two others to bring the Lawrence children back to New York City. Ranging from 2 to 13 years old, the children stayed with sympathetic working-class families. (For more information on this radical labor organization, enter "IWW" into any search engine and browse the sites listed.)

Arriving in Lawrence on February 10, Sanger presented the perfect public relations image. She was educated; she was a nurse; and she was attractive. She carefully documented the ragged and deplorable condition of all 119 children. Though their parents, and sometimes the children themselves, worked in woolen mills, no child wore any wool clothing. Only 4 wore underwear; only

20 had overcoats. One child had just recovered from chicken pox; another gone to work infected with diphtheria.

Sanger took the children away by train. In New York City, an enthusiastic crowd met Sanger and the children, breaking through the police lines and hoisting the children to their shoulders. The group formed a parade, complete with a band, torches, and banners. They took the children to be fed and introduced to their foster parents. Sanger had moved from the street corners to the newspapers.

Lawrence police stopped a second exodus of children, arresting and clubbing both children and their mothers. Shocked by such brutality, a Socialist congressman held hearings in the House of Representatives. Along with 50 others, Sanger testified, referring to the detailed notes she had kept on each child. She told the committee the children were "very much emaciated; every child there showed the effects of malnutrition." [51]

News coverage intensified when both President William Howard Taft's wife and Alice Roosevelt, the daughter of former president Theodore Roosevelt, attended the hearings. Unable to overcome this bad publicity, the mill owners gave in to the strikers' demands on March 12. Their success encouraged other unions to follow and use direct action to achieve their goals.

Four months later, Sanger's life would change forever. Hospitals, in the early 1900s, were regarded suspiciously, and most babies were born at home. Sanger narrowed her nursing cases to delivering babies. She had many cases, and working in the Lower East Side, she tended the very poor and very uneducated, people who were never helped by any charitable organization. "Pregnancy was a chronic condition among the women of this class," she wrote. "I could not escape from the factors of their wretchedness; neither was I able to see any way out." [52] There were simply wasn't anything legal or inexpensive that a poor woman could employ to keep from getting pregnant. State laws prohibited publication of contraceptive information. The Comstock laws said that sex was a personal matter and not a topic discussed by "decent" people. Doctors believed women couldn't be trusted to make an important decision like family planning.

A **diaphragm**, a contraceptive device consisting of a flexible dome-shaped cup, had to be internally fitted by a doctor and cost money the poor didn't have. Other contraceptive measures were illegal, including pessaries, suppositories, sponges that were inserted in the vagina to destroy sperm, and douches to flush the sperm out of the vagina. They could, however, be bought for the right price from both legal and illegal sources. Men often didn't care how many pregnancies resulted from sex. **Condoms**, thin rubber sheaths worn over the penis during intercourse, were available for men, primarily those who visited prostitutes. Because condoms were associated with prostitutes, women wouldn't mention them to their husbands. Poor women were left to the only contraception available to them: abortion. **Abortion**, the termination of a pregnancy through an artificial procedure, was illegal too. Women without means had few options beyond attempting the procedure themselves (often via an instrument as crude as a coat hanger) or relying on "back alley" physicians, many of whom did not use sanitary procedures.

One day in mid-July 1912, Jake Sachs found his wife, Sadie, on the floor of their three-room apartment. She had collapsed from an attempted abortion. He hurriedly called for a physician. Sanger came with the doctor to help treat the resulting blood poisoning. Sanger stayed with her for three weeks. When the doctor made his last visit, Sadie asked him how she could prevent another pregnancy. His cold-hearted response brought Sanger to tears and Sadie to despair.

"You want to have your cake and eat it too, do you? Well, it can't be done," he said. "Tell Jake to sleep on the roof." [53]

After he left, Sadie turned to Sanger. "He can't understand. He's only a man," she said. "But you do, don't you? Please tell me the secret, and I'll never breathe it to a soul. Please." [54]

Sanger had no answer for her. She made Sadie comfortable and left. Three months later, Sanger received a phone call from Jake Sachs, begging her to save his wife from another self-induced abortion. She had fallen into a coma. This time, Sanger couldn't help her. Sadie never came out of her coma and died.

Sanger was deeply moved by Sadie's needless death and thought about the desperate circumstances that caused it. She later wrote "pain and grief crowded in upon me. . . women writhing in travail to bring forth little babies; the babies themselves naked and hungry, wrapped in newspapers to keep them from the cold, six-year-old children with pinched, pale, wrinkled faces . . . I could bear it no longer. I knew I could not go back to merely keeping people alive."[55]

Margaret Sanger had found her destiny. She quit urging women to vote or organize a union or strike for increased wages. She resolved to "change the destiny of mothers whose miseries were vast as the sky."[56]

Scenes from the Life
of Margaret Sanger

Anne Purcell Higgins, Margaret's mother, was the epitome of everything Margaret hated about what society expected of women. She spent her days doing household chores, she never argued with her husband, and she was pregnant 18 times in 22 years.

Michael Higgins, Margaret's father. Michael was a stonemason by trade and a political firebrand, whose ideas on social justice evidently influenced his daughter. He lost work with church cemeteries because of his outspoken atheism and defiance of church authority, and the family's finances suffered heavily.

Young Margaret Louisa Higgins (left), with three of her sisters: Mary, Nan, and Ethel. Margaret was the sixth child and third daughter of Anne Purcell Higgins and Michael Higgins.

William Sanger, a 28-year-old architect, met Margaret by chance, and within six months convinced her to marry him. This forced Margaret to give up her nurse's training, something she always regretted.

Stuart, Peggy, and Grant Sanger—Sanger's children—in Paris, 1913.

The Brownsville Clinic, opened by Margaret Sanger at 46 Amboy Street, Brooklyn, in 1916, was America's first birth control clinic. Although controversial, the clinic offered women information on limiting their families for the first time. Such information had always been available to women who could afford to pay a physician.

Margaret Sanger and her sister, Ethel Byrne, at Sanger's court hearing. The courts tried Sanger for sending her book *The Woman Rebel* through the mail.

Delegates attending America's first birth-control conference, 1925. Sanger organized the Neo-Malthusian and Birth Control Conference, held at the Hotel McAlpin in New York in 1925. Margaret Sanger is shown third from the right.

Margaret Sanger with second husband Noah Slee, in the Alps, 1927–1928. Slee, a billionaire and conservative "pillar of society," felt that Sanger filled a void in his life. He contributed heavily to Sanger's causes and stood by her side during her trials.

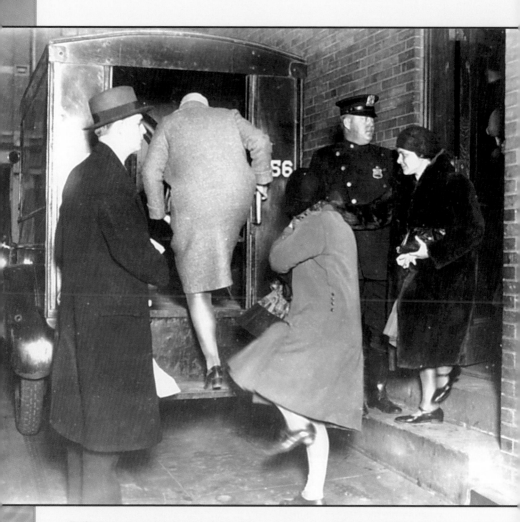

Police prepare to haul away eight staff members, including two physicians, of the Birth Control Clinical Research Bureau, on April 15, 1929. The charges, levied by an undercover policewoman, were later dropped.

Gregory Pincus (left), M.D., with General William F. Draper (center) and Cass Canfield (right), were all instrumental in the development and promotion of the birth control pill. Pincus invented it, Draper convinced President Eisenhower to make family planning aid available to other governments, and Canfield served as chairman of the board of the Planned Parenthood Federation from 1959–1962.

Margaret Sanger escorted by Prime Minister Jawaharlal Nehru at the 6th International Planned Parenthood Conference, New Delhi, India, in 1959. Sanger had met Nehru several times before, but this time he pledged his support as well as $10 million for family planning in India.

Although the last years of Sanger's life were marked with increased frailty and declining health, she continued to fight for the causes she believed in, traveling to Japan and India to attend conferences. She is shown here in 1959, at 80 years of age.

4

The Rebel
Speaks Out

After Sanger's successful series, "How Six little Children were Told the Truth," Anita Block asked her to write another series on health and sex education. Block prepared readers for reading "What Every Girl Should Know" by saying, "We want to keep girls, who do not know the nature and meaning of their sex impulses, from being victimized by weak and unscrupulous men. . . . Where are our readers to get such information . . . if not here?"[57]

The twelve-part series, running from November 17, 1912 through March 2, 1913, was to explain female sexuality from puberty to menopause. Sanger's first columns caused a firestorm. The subject was the forbidden topic of sex, and written by a woman at that. Letters ranged from praise to outrage. "Every reader owes Margaret Sanger a debt of appreciation," said one. Another said she "blushed" but found the articles "indicative of a higher, purer morality than whole libraries full of hypocritical cant about modesty."[58] Others wrote that *The Call* was "polluted" and had been "banished from our home circle."[59]

Sanger's February 9, 1913, column discussed **venereal diseases**, communicable diseases transmitted by sexual intercourse. She matter-of-factly defined the diseases **syphilis** and **gonorrhea**, and described their effects on both men and women. Still the political radical, she concluded writing, "Until capitalism is swept away, there is no hope for young girls to live a beautiful life during their girlhood."[60] This time, it appeared that she had gone too far. Using the Comstock laws, which banned sending material about sexually transmitted diseases through the mail, the post office seized issues of *The Call*. Anita Block did not take the censorship quietly. She printed the next issue with an empty box in place of Sanger's column and the headline, "What Every Girl Should Know—*Nothing* by order of the Post Office Department."[61] The public forgot its opposition to Sanger's subject in its anger that *The Call* had been censored, violating the First Amendment's guarantee of free speech.

Readers wrote sympathetic letters to *The Call*. A socialist newspaper denounced the seizure and a socialist congressman asked for an investigation. Eventually the column was published. Its explanations were so clear that the War and Navy Departments later reprinted them (without Sanger's permission) in pamphlets for the military personnel during World War I. It would be revised, translated into several languages, and remain in print until 1980.

The "What Every Young Girl Should Know" incident was the first round of a vicious war between Margaret Sanger and **Anthony Comstock**, the enforcer of oppressive obscenity laws. Two weeks after Comstock banned her column, Sanger was deep into the Paterson, New Jersey, silk mill workers' strike. She

The Comstock Laws

Anthony Comstock was obsessed with obscenity. In 1873, after getting a New York State statute prohibiting traffic in contraception and abortion, he showed up at Congressional committee hearings to campaign for similar federal laws. He lumped contraceptive and anti-abortion devices together with pornographic material and told the Congressmen that all these things were lowering the nation's morals. Few politicians would argue against saving the nation's morals, so the Comstock Act became law. It was passed, along with 260 other bills, on the last day of the Congressional session. The Comstock Act outlawed anything that could be used for "preventing conception or producing abortion or for any indecent or immoral purpose." It did not define what "indecent" and "immoral" were. The Comstock Act also barred "any article of an immoral nature, or any drug or medicine or any article whatever for the prevention of conception" from distribution through the United States postal system.

While controlling obscenity was admirable, the danger in Comstock's laws was that they provided no guidelines for left her writing, nursing, and her family to walk the picket lines and speak to the women strikers.

She appeared at a rally with the IWW's leader, "Big Bill" Haywood and spoke about the woman's right to limit family size. Haywood followed her on the podium. He completely contradicted everything she said, speaking about a future where women "could have without fear of want all the babies they pleased."[62] Like the Socialists, her direct action comrade had discounted the importance of limiting family size. Sanger was disappointed at his lack of support.

While the Paterson strike continued, Sanger was sent by the IWW leaders to Hazleton, Pennsylvania, to help striking silk

defining what was obscene. A "filthy book, pamphlet, picture, paper" could be virtually anything.

Individuals convicted of violating the act could receive up to five years of imprisonment with hard labor and a fine of up to $2,000. With a federal law in place, 14 states passed laws against talking about contraception or abortion.

Comstock was appointed special agent and enforcer of the law. Without any federal guidelines and definitions, he was the only one who decided what was obscene and what wasn't. Comstock went to work. He arrested store owners who left naked mannequins in their windows and tried to ban art books that showed nudes. He attacked George Bernard Shaw's play, "Mrs. Warren's Profession." He wrote letters pretending to be a woman and pleading for advice on family limitation. He arrested any physicians who wrote back with birth control advice. One physician was sentenced to seven years in prison. Comstock especially liked pouncing on strong-minded and vocal feminists. Margaret Sanger fit those categories perfectly.

workers there. Margaret Sanger, the quiet matron had been replaced by Margaret Sanger, the activist. She strongly objected to her arrests on April 8 and 9 for "loitering" as she walked the picket line. Newspaper accounts say she took a swing at a Hazleton alderman and then threatened to "slap"[63] his face. She was sentenced to five days in jail.

The Call published her descriptions of her jail time. Her grim cell had iron walls and a toilet that was flushed once a day. She had no blankets, towel, or soap. She was allowed two cups of water each day for drinking and washing. But the grim surroundings did not squash Sanger's or the picketers' spirit. Her fellow demonstrators sang revolutionary songs and banged on the walls all night. A comrade smashed the water pitcher after a cockroach was discovered in it. Others emptied their filthy toilets with their drinking cups, sending a stream of sewage into the major's office in the next room.

Sanger was fired up and ready to remake the world. She declared, "There is something now to work for, to live for. It is the fight to emancipate the worker from wage slavery."[64] But her enthusiasm did not last. The strike organizers planned a grand pageant in New York City to dramatize the strikers' plight. They met at the Sangers' house to plan the June 7 event. Sanger led the parade to Madison Square Garden. Unfortunately, the pageant failed as a fund-raising event. The public did not stand behind the Paterson workers as it had for the Lawrence workers. Eventually, the strike ended in July with no gains for the workers. Its failure thoroughly depressed Sanger, and she moved further away from radical causes and organizations.

Political causes were not the only thing disturbing Sanger. She increasingly wanted a life beyond her husband and children. Bill no longer agreed with her radical ideas. Tension rose in their marriage. In effect, Sanger left it emotionally, though the marriage officially continued until 1921. A writer, Hutchins Hapgood, recalled the couple at the time. Bill was "a sweet gentle painter who lacked ego and ambition" and one to whom "his pretty wife . . . seemed to grant little value."[65]

That summer, she vacationed in Provincetown, Massachusetts, with Stuart, Grant, and Peggy. While the children played at the beach, Sanger mulled over the tragedy of Sadie Sachs, wondering what more she could do. Leaving the children with her sister, Ethel, she traveled to the Boston Public Library to learn more about contraceptive procedures. Material was available, but she discovered the information wasn't written in simple enough language for the average person to comprehend.

While at Provincetown, Big Bill Haywood suggested Sanger visit the more enlightened atmosphere of France to investigate contraception and family limitation trends further. Her husband also liked the idea, because the trip would provide him with the opportunity to paint in the company of revolutionary French artists. He also hoped having more time with Margaret would help their marriage.

The Sangers left for France on October 17, 1913, stopping first in Glasgow, Scotland, so Margaret could report on its Socialist government for *The Call*. Upon arriving in Paris, Bill headed for the artist district, while Margaret talked to French supporters of family limitation. She learned the poor limited the number of children they had because heirs split any inheritance equally. To Sanger, this seemed a more practical way of solving society's problems than all the strikes and unrest the American Socialists and labor groups stirred up. She agreed with the French belief that women should be in charge of social change. She also liked their idea that sex was not indecent, but an important part of a loving relationship. She bought samples of French diaphragms and pessaries to take back to the States. Three months into the trip, Margaret had "reached the exploding point. I could not contain my ideas," she said. "I wanted to get on with what I had to do in the world."[66]

On December 24, 1913, she and the children boarded a ship for the United States; Bill remained in Paris to paint. Any hope for their marriage disappeared as the ship sailed out of sight. While Bill continually declared his love for her in his letters, Margaret believed the marriage was over. Just like her father, Bill no longer supported his wife and family. In fact, Margaret supported his artistic life with the rental payments from their Hastings-On-Hudson property and with her earnings. She asked Bill to release her "physically and spiritually"[67] from their marriage. This in itself was scandalous because at the turn of the century, there were only 20 divorces per 10,000 couples. Bill pleaded with her to consider their past together and their responsibilities towards their children. But the more he pleaded, the more determined she was leave him.

Besides achieving control over her life, Margaret had a new project. On her way back from France, she decided to put out a monthly newspaper, *The Woman Rebel*. Once home, she planned for three months. She tried to get Heterodoxy Club, a feminist group in New York City, to give her financial and emotional support for *The Woman Rebel*. It declined to help her, thinking she was an uneducated, emotional radical. Advertisements in several radical journals, however, resulted in 200 subscriptions and enough money to begin the publication.

She called it *The Woman Rebel* because "I believe that woman is enslaved by the world machine, by sex conventions, by motherhood, and its necessary childbearing, by wage slavery, by middle-class morality."[68] The front page of each issue challenged America's working women "to look the world in the face with a go-to-hell look in the eyes."[69] Sanger wanted to provide women with contraceptive information and stir them to action. More importantly, she wanted to challenge the Comstock laws. A few friends volunteered to help her launch the magazine. They all agreed the movement needed a new name. "Family limitation" and "voluntary motherhood" were too awkward to say. During a meeting at her modest apartment, one friend suggested **birth control**. Sanger liked the word "control" because it implied women's power over reproduction. The phrase was to stay.

The Woman Rebel's first issue, in March 1914, was immediately and unfairly banned by the Post Office. It had not printed any contraceptive information, but had simply reminded its readers of the laws against giving out contraceptive information and asked if it was not time to defy them. While four subsequent issues were seized, seven other issues made it to 5,000 subscribers and the various labor organizations that Sanger added to the mailing list without charge. Sanger discovered that by putting one or two copies of the publication in individual mailboxes throughout the city, instead of mailing bundles of magazines from a post office, the magazine was processed and mailed. She and her volunteers walked around all night, mailing them.

The June issue revealed what would become Sanger's lifelong motto: "A woman's body belongs to herself alone. It does not belong to the church. It does not belong to the United States of America. . . . The first step towards getting life, liberty and the pursuit of happiness for any woman is her decision whether or not she shall become a mother. Enforced motherhood is the most complete denial of a woman's right to life and liberty."[70] Reaction to *The Woman Rebel* was strong. One newspaper said that it was "a mass of dirty slush."[71] A radical publication, *The Masses*, criticized Sanger's rabble-rousing style and tone. It suggested that reasonable people might be more influenced by a quieter approach to the issues. Her brothers and sisters thought she had experienced a nervous breakdown. Her father, who had come to convince her to stop her activities, was with her when two Justice Department agents served her papers. Sanger charmed them into talking about birth control. Listening to them, he told her, "If your mother had only known about birth control, she'd be alive today."[72]

In August 1914, she was indicted on three counts of publishing obscenities and one count of advocating assassination. Her court date was set for October. She decided if she were to be tried for breaking the Comstock laws, she might as well really break them. Instead of preparing for her court case, she wrote a 16-page pamphlet called *Family Limitation*. Her advice was very straightforward. She urged women to know about their bodies. She advised them about methods of feminine hygiene and keeping track of their menstrual cycle. She used diagrams of the current, if illegal, contraceptives and evaluated each. She recommended the pessary as the most effective.

Printers wouldn't touch it. One said, "I'd like to set it, but I have a family. I'd be in jail the minute it came out."[73] She approached as many as twenty before finding a Russian immigrant who secretly printed 100,000 copies after his day job was finished.

Sanger knew that she could be sentenced to 45 years in prison and fined thousands of dollars for distributing the publication. Thinking that her fate in court was already determined, she made a startling decision. She later said "the only thing I could do was set sail for Europe, prepare my case adequately, stay until the war was over, and return then to fight it out in the courts...."[74] Sanger left her children without saying good-bye and took a train to Montreal. Then with a false passport under the name of Bertha Watson, she sailed for Europe. After three days at sea, she cabled her volunteers to mail out and distribute through the IWW members and other sympathetic groups all 100,000 copies of *Family Limitation*. She had broken the Comstock laws again.

The Rebel
Steps Out

5

From October 14, 1914, when she sailed for Europe, until her return a year later, Sanger learned much about loneliness and homesickness, much about contraception, and much about passion.

She arrived in England during World War I. Her new life was just as dark as the London streets. Wary of air raids, people were tense and suspicious of strangers. She had little money with her and would have no income except for what her friends sent from sales of "What Every Young Girl Should Know" and *Family Limitation*. Sometimes they sent donations from activist organizations. All Sanger could afford was an unheated, third-floor apartment. She paid extra for using the bathroom. Sometimes when she couldn't stand the cold any more, she splurged and rented a room downstairs with a fireplace to study more comfortably.

At first, she was desperately lonely for her children. In her dreams, she heard Peggy crying, "Mother, Mother, are you coming back?"[75] The number 6 recurred in her nightmares. The letter she wrote to a 4-year-old who wanted her mother was hardly comforting. "I would weep from loneliness for you—just to touch your soft chubby hands . . . but work is to be done, dear—work to make your path easier—and those who come after you."[76]

In New York City, Grant and Peggy stayed with family friends while their father worked. Usually bright-eyed and bubbly, Peggy cried after him, thinking he would disappear like her mother. Could she, she asked, "fly to her mother on wings?"[77] Wistfully, Stuart, 11, wrote Sanger from boarding school, "I would have sent you some [flowers from the school's garden] but "you are so far away."[78]

But Sanger soon realized without her family, she could concentrate on contraception research and make new friends. Though at first unsure about the feisty American, British birth control campaigners were surprised to meet a "soft-voiced, gentle mannered, altogether charming 'rebel'."[79] They soon accepted her and let her use their personal libraries when she was not spending 10 hours a day at the British Museum. She visited with intellectuals gathered at cafes, just as she and Bill had done in New York City.

She also began a love affair. On December 22, 1914, she met Havelock Ellis, who had written a seven-volume series about the psychology of sex. The first time they met, both were immediately attracted to each other. They talked for hours about writing difficulties, getting published, and their life experiences. Sanger overwhelmed the shy psychologist. The tall, white-bearded man with the thick white hair was completely taken by her. Ellis guided her research and reading in the British Museum. He took her to concerts and introduced her to famous writers like H.G. Wells. He suggested she soften the shrill tone of her writing. "It is no use . . . smashing your head against a brick wall," he told her, "for not one rebel, or even many rebels, can crush law by force."[80] (For more information on this influencial psychologist, enter "Havelock Ellis" into any search engine and browse the sites listed.)

Back home, more controversy swirled around the Sanger name. This time, on January 19, 1915, it was Bill Sanger who was arrested. Sanger had given his one copy of *Family Limitation* to a man who came to his art studio. The next day, the man returned, accompanied by a large man with mutton chop whiskers. "I am Mr. Comstock," he said. "I have a warrant for your arrest."[81]

Authorities told Sanger if he revealed Margaret's whereabouts, he would get off easier. Bill was not about to betray the woman he still loved. He told them, "You can wait till hell freezes over before that will happen."[82] His trial was set for September 1915. He believed his arrest was just bait to bring Margaret home to five years in prison, and Margaret had no intention of walking into that trap.

In February, with introductory letters from Havelock, Margaret Sanger traveled to see Holland's government-supported birth control clinics. Dutch women's death rate from pregnancies was the lowest in the world, three times lower than that in the United States.[83] Originally, Sanger had thought women could teach each other how to use contraceptives or learn by reading pamphlets. The doctors and nurses in the Dutch clinics changed her mind. In these clinics, Dutch women learned about every type of female contraception: the diaphragm, sponges, suppositories with quinine, and douching. The clinics recommended diaphragms, since the woman was responsible for its use and her partner didn't even know it was in place. The clinics included follow-up services to track the effectiveness of each method. Sanger would use the

Female Contraceptive Devices

Before Margaret Sanger's crusade, few poor women knew that **contraceptives,** devices that prevent conception, existed. Since middle-class and wealthy women could pay for a doctor's appointment, they could obtain information about contraceptives. They could find, and pay for, the devices illegally. In the late 19th and early 20th century, however, choices of contraception for women were limited, and existing methods were less than perfect. **Abortion,** the premature termination of a pregnancy, induced by herbs or manipulation, was widely used as a method of birth control, although most abortions in the United States had been outlawed by the end of the 19th century.

Although the **condom,** a device that covers a man's penis during sexual intercourse, was available to men, pessaries and diaphragms were among the only contraceptive methods that a woman could use to prevent pregnancy. The **pessary** is a rubber ring that was invented to support a uterus or bladder that had slipped out of position. This condition usually resulted from having multiple pregnancies, which stretched the muscles

Dutch procedures in her own clinics. In a class for midwifes, she learned how to fit diaphragms, fitting 75 women herself. Coming from the United States, where it was illegal to even talk about contraception, Sanger was amazed that in Holland, the purchase of a diaphragm "was looked upon as no more unusual than we in America look upon the purchase of a toothbrush."[84]

Though not all Dutch doctors appreciated talking to "just a nurse," Dr. Johannes Rutgers called Sanger's *Family Limitation* "a brilliant pamphlet."[85] In the United States, the judge in charge of Bill's trial thought differently. His opinion mirrored many others. During the September 10,

holding the uterus in place. Since a pessary blocks the opening to the cervix, it also is somewhat effective in preventing sperm from reaching its destination. Used at the turn of the century, the pessary is not a recommended birth control device today and is used primarily for female incontinence, or urinary leakage.

Dr. Wilhelm Mensinga invented the **diaphragm** in the 1880s. It is a rubber dome-shaped disk that blocks sperm from entering the uterus. It is typically used with a **spermicide**, an agent that kills sperm. It needs to be fitted correctly by a physician after an internal examination and is only available by prescription. When used properly, it is 96–98 percent effective.

The **cervical cap** is a smaller, more modern version of the diaphragm. The thimble-sized apparatus is inserted in the vagina and fits over the cervix. Suction keeps it secure. It also requires a spermicide. If used correctly, the cervical cap is 91 percent effective.

1915 trial, the judge described *Family Limitation* as "not only contrary to the laws of the State but contrary to the laws of God. Any man or woman who would circulate literature of this kind is a menace to the community."[86] He believed if women concentrated on bearing children instead of on women's issues, that this city and society would be better off."[87]

The judge gave Bill a choice between a $150 fine or a 30-day jail sentence. Bill replied, "I would rather be in jail with my self-respect than in your place without it."[88] Spectators in the courtroom cheered. Speaking to reporters from his prison cell, Bill called his sentence "a modern martyrdom to Comstockian prudery and ignorance."[89]

Margaret Sanger returned to the United States October 6, 1915, after a year away from the headlines. She rushed to see Grant and Peggy, then staying with friends, and to see Stuart in boarding school. She may have been jealous that her husband had replaced her in the news. She didn't visit Bill, who was serving the last of his sentence. He only learned she'd returned through friends.

On returning, Sanger discovered birth control was no longer an unmentionable topic. The New York Academy of Medicine held informal discussions about contraception. Mary Ware Dennett had founded the National Birth Control League, an organization promoting change through peaceful legislation, rather than through public and militant confrontations. Magazines included articles and editorials about contraception. One conducted a contest for the best explanation for practicing birth control. Most importantly, influential and wealthy women who needed a "cause" began supporting the birth control movement.

None of this meant anything to Sanger four weeks later. Her world suddenly crashed down around her when her 5-year-old daughter Peggy died of pneumonia in her arms on November 6. The family was shattered. Grant kept saying his best friend wouldn't have died if her mother had been there. Stuart was in despair. Bill, like Margaret's father once did, made a sculpture of his daughter's body. Margaret went to pieces. "The days after Peggy died were the darkest days of my life,"[90] she said. Sanger never fully recovered. She attended seances trying to reach Peggy beyond the grave. For a long time, she couldn't look at a 5-year-old without crying. Everything on the anniversary of Peggy's death stopped while she mourned.

Sanger received thousands of sympathy letters from *The Woman Rebel* readers, political activists, and the laborers she had helped. Some enclosed money. Others told sad stories of losing their own children. Rather than go mad with grief, Sanger returned to the cause. Sanger still wanted to challenge the Comstock laws in court. Since other publications discussing birth control hadn't been prosecuted, she wrote the U.S. district attorney, asking if she was still indicted. He proposed she plead guilty, pay a fine, and end the issue. Her lawyer said she wouldn't have to go to court if she promised not to break the law again. "I'm not concerned about going to jail," she said. "The question is whether I have or have not done something obscene."[91] Sanger went to court.

Sanger knew publicity was almost as important as the trial itself. She planned to wear a black skirt, white shirt, and a man's necktie. John Reed, a friend from her Socialist days, suggested a softer look in a publicity photograph, and she agreed. The woman who posed in a lace-collared dress was no hard-nosed troublemaker. Stuart stood beside her, and Grant leaned into her lap. Their faces were still ravaged with the grief of Peggy's passing. The photo ran across the country. Sympathy and money poured in from upper class society.

Her new wealthy friends hosted a pre-trial dinner for her at the Hotel Brevoort. She told them, "There is nothing new and radical about birth control. Aristotle and Plato advocated it."[92] She admitted her behavior had been too radical in the past and hoped that others, like them, could act better. The audience loved her humility, and many pledged more financial support.

But Sanger's case never went to trial. After two postponements, the government dropped the charges on February 18. The district attorney explained that the case was two years old and "Mrs. Sanger was not a disorderly person."[93] He seemed, however, to have an ulterior motive in dropping the case, saying later, "We are not the least bit interested in having a public debate on sex theories at this time."[94]

Riding high on her new celebrity status and the public's sympathy and support, Sanger hit the road on a three-month speaking tour. Starting on April 7, 1916, she traveled to nineteen cities, lecturing 119 times to mixed receptions. She spoke in Pittsburgh and Cleveland, where she set up birth control leagues. In Chicago, 1,500 women attended her lecture, where some critics called her literature "too brutal." Like her father's experience years before, the Catholic Church locked her out of a building in St. Louis. She counterattacked by charging her right to free speech had been violated. The St. Louis City Men's Club then asked her to speak. More people attended her speech than had attended Theodore Roosevelt's speech there. In June, three weeks later, she was arrested in Portland, Oregon, and spent the night in jail. Her crime was distributing *Family Limitation*. The uproar she inspired made birth control one of the media's hottest topics.

Sanger returned from the tour ready to open America's first birth control clinic. Sixteen days after it opened, Sanger, Ethel Byrne, and Fania Mindell were arrested, setting the scene for the cause's long-awaited day in court. Ethel's trial came first, on January 4, 1917. Women from every level of society supported her. Members of the Committee of One Hundred, a group of wealthy socialites were there. Rose Halpern, a "poorly clad"[95] mother of six, came as a "demonstration"[96] of the need for the poor to receive birth control information. Subpoenaed to testify, several Brownsville Clinic patients were there. Children played at their mother's feet. Babies squalled when they were hungry or needed changing. The spectators violently clapped when Ethel's lawyer argued that Section 1142 of New York's Comstock law was unconstitutional.

In the end, Ethel was convicted of distributing birth control information. The issue was not over. Sanger and Ethel planned a daring publicity stunt. Sentenced to 30 days in Blackwell's Island workhouse, Ethel declared, "I intend to go on a hunger strike . . . They may force me to eat, but if they do it will be because I may be too weak to resist them."[97] Like Margaret Sanger, Ethel hardly looked like a criminal. "Everything in her voice and manner suggested gentleness," a reporter said.[98]

Her fast began on a Monday, January 22, 1917, at 6 o'clock. As hours stretched to days, her story made front-page news. On January 26, Ethel was quoted on the *New York Times* front page. "With the Health Department reporting 8,000 deaths a year in the state from illegal operations on women, one more death won't make much difference, anyway," she said.[99] In the meantime, her attorney appeared before New York Supreme Court arguing again that the law that convicted Ethel was unconstitutional. The district attorney argued that the birth control "propaganda had come into the possession of high school girls and others of tender age"[100] and that the clinic threatened the community.

As Ethel weakened without food or water, prison officials released accounts of her vital signs. By January 27, force-feeding was being discussed. Sanger, denied access to her sister, made the news saying, "Officialism is running riot, when one sister is not permitted to see another who is in a dying condition."[101] The next day, Ethel was wrapped tightly in a blanket, a tube forced down her throat, and she was fed eggs, brandy, and milk.

In a war of publicity, the workhouse commissioner said Ethel was near normal. Sanger claimed Ethel had lapsed into a coma. The commissioner countered with doctor's reports. Sanger and the Committee of One Hundred held a rally at Carnegie Hall at which 3,000 people attended. Working women paid 25¢ for the upper seats. Wealthy women sat in the box seats. For dramatic effect, Sanger suggested some Brownsville Clinic clients be seated on the stage. The event raised $1,000.

Sanger utilized flaming rhetoric, saying, "I come to you tonight from a crowded courtroom, from a vortex of persecution. I come not from the stake of Salem, where women were burned for blasphemy, but from the shadow of Blackwell's Island where women are tortured for obscenity. . . . No woman can call herself free until she can choose the time she will become a mother."[102] The audience cheered wildly. "I never saw another meeting like it," said one attendee. "She had it—the power of a saint combined with the mind of a statesman. I realized that night she was one of the great women of our time."[103]

By Wednesday, January 31, members of the Committee of One Hundred became alarmed at Ethel's condition. They took Sanger to New York Governor Charles Whitman, requesting he pardon Ethel and appoint a commission to study birth control. He insisted Ethel promise never to break the law again. Ethel refused. Then Sanger saw how delirious Ethel had become. Alarmed, she declared Ethel was unable to speak for herself and accepted the Governor's condition for her.

Ethel's sentence was commuted after serving 10 days. She was carried on a stretcher from the prison. Ethel was never again active in her sister's cause. Some theorize that Sanger was jealous of her sister's celebrity; others think

Ethel honored Sanger's promise to the governor. Still others believe Ethel clashed with Sanger about welcoming wealthy socialites into the cause. Sanger's strategy was clear. "We cannot doubt that they and they alone dominate when they get an interest in a thing," she told Ethel. "So little can be done without them."[104]

6

The Rebel
Evolves

On January 29, 1917, Margaret Sanger arrived for her trial dressed in her proper hat and gloves. She carried a bouquet of American Beauty roses her wealthy friends had given her. Thirty women from the Brownsville Clinic with their children, diapers, and sack lunches crowded into the courtroom. Members of the Committee of One Hundred sat nearby.

The prosecutors thought testimony by the Brownsville women would incriminate Sanger. Instead, they reported that Sanger had helped them "stop the babies."[105] Their heartbreaking stories of past miscarriages, illness, and dying children caused one judge to adjourn court, saying, "I can't stand this any longer."[106]

Certain Sanger would appeal her conviction, the judges offered her a lenient sentence if she promised not to break the law again. "I cannot respect the law as it exists today,"[107] she replied. Spectators cheered and clapped. Sanger chose 30 days in the workhouse over the $5,000 fine. When sentence was read, a supporter of Sanger shouted, "Shame."[108] Citing her health, Sanger announced she would not repeat her sister's hunger strike.

She was admitted to Queens County jail, February 7, 1917. Claiming she was not a convicted criminal, Sanger refused to be fingerprinted or submit to a physical examination.

She served her sentence quietly. She talked with women prisoners about birth control, taught them how to read, and answered mail from Ethel, Stuart, Grant, and supporters. She finally realized that acceptance for birth control would not come from "direct action" protests or by legislative process. She realized the hope of the movement lay with wealthy women who could use their wealth and influence to change public opinion.

Sanger was released March 6, 1917, after a bruising, two-hour struggle against officials who attempted to fingerprint her. The large crowd who greeted her and the inmates who hung out the windows sang the rousing French national anthem. She went to lunch at a hotel, given in her honor by her wealthy friends. She had a Turkish bath and attended the theater. She told reporters, "Already I feel ready to begin work again."[109]

Though her sisters and a new suitor who wanted to marry her helped her out, Sanger virtually had no money. Her immediate problem was finding a place to live. She located a tiny apartment without heat or hot water. The bathtub was in the kitchen; the bedroom was just big enough for a bed and a dresser. Sanger's second priority was her new magazine, *The Birth Control Review*. Remembering Havelock Ellis's advice, she toned down her revolutionary language to educate, rather than agitate, readers. Helping her was Frederick Blossom, a young Socialist Party worker from Cleveland, who maintained the magazine during her trial preparations.

Beginning February 1917, the magazine included articles on Ethel's hunger strike, existing prison conditions, and the dangers of overpopulation. It advertised Sanger's speaking schedule and printed wrenching letters from poor women. Later, friends and birth control advocates like H.G. Wells and Havelock Ellis wrote for *The Review*.

Several thousand subscribers, newsstand sales, and benefactors supported *The Review*. Sanger and her friends sold copies on street corners. Some passersby bought the magazine; others yelled and spit at them. "You vile creature, you ought to bury your face in the mud, you dirty thing!" one woman told Sanger, before knocking magazines out of her hands.[110]

Blossom was a good organizer, but the handsome and educated man threatened Sanger's leadership. By the third issue of *The Birth Control Review*, he and Sanger clashed. She wrote an editorial arguing that overpopulation and overcrowding inspired Germany's invasion of other countries. Blossom wouldn't run it. Sanger opened the office door one morning to find Blossom had taken furniture and files of 2,000 subscribers and left discrepancies in the budget. Out of money, *The Birth Control Review* survived only because Sanger's friends stepped in. One friend, Juliet Rublee, paid the office rent, gave Sanger money to live on, and incorporated the magazine into the New York Women's Publishing Company.

After the United States declared war on Germany on April 2, 1917, pro-war sentiments clashed with civil liberties. Sanger's Socialist friends, Eugene Debs, Big Bill Haywood, and Emma Goldman, were imprisoned for protesting the war. The Sedition Act of 1918 made it unlawful to use "disloyal, profane, scurrilous, or abusive" language to describe the government, Constitution, flag, or military. It gave the government free rein to crack down on critics. Sanger, the protester and activist, escaped the witch-hunt. She angered Blossom's Socialist friends by asking the district attorney to investigate him. They censured her. Ironically, being censured by the Socialists, along with the embrace of her cause by socialites, made Sanger respectable.

January 8, 1918, was a triumphant day for Margaret Sanger. Judge Frederick E. Crane of the New York Court of Appeals ruled on her Brownsville trial. Though he upheld her conviction, he rejected Comstock's narrow interpretation of the word "disease." He overruled Section 1145's edict that physicians could only prescribe contraception to cure and to prevent the spread of venereal disease. He ruled that they could legally prescribe contraceptives for any condition that threatened the client's health.

Margaret Sanger and the Crane decision triumphed over Anthony Comstock. But the movement took all her energies. She was devoted to Stuart and Grant when she had the time, swimming and horseback riding with them. She just rarely had the time to be devoted. Once Stuart walked 10 miles to the railroad station to meet her. She didn't show up. Grant's letters pleaded for her attention. In February he wrote from boarding school, "I know you are very busy, or you would come and see me." Later he asked, "Am I coming home for Easter? Write and tell me so, please." Near Thanksgiving he wrote, "Now you put down in your engagement book, 'Nov. 28, Go down to see Grant!'"[111] Sanger wrote him to go to her apartment, where she said that her maid would make him dinner.

Straightening out *The Birth Control Review* and maneuvering through the infighting with other birth control supporters took their toll. Sanger was plagued by fatigue, weight loss, and

Crackdown on Civil Liberties

The United States decision, in April 1917, to join the Allies in World War I brought not just military mobilization but also a rise in patriotism and hatred of all things German. Hostility also arose against those who had opposed the war. Many of those who had opposed the war were reformers and Socialist Party leaders.

Intolerance for dissent from the mainstream took legal form in the Sedition Act of 1918, which made it unlawful to use "disloyal, profane, scurrilous, or abusive language" about the government, Constitution, flag, or military. The government used this measure to crack down on critics in general, arresting over 1,500 Socialists, pacifists, and others who spoke out against the war. Socialist Party leader Eugene V. Debs was arrested and given a 10-year sentence for delivering a speech supporting the right to criticize the government. Emma Goldman, an anarchist and birth control reformer, was arrested in 1917 for conspiring to obstruct the draft and was sentenced to two years.

In the last few months of the war, American hatred for Germany transferred to hatred of Russia, which had just undergone a Communist revolution. This led to a further backlash against American radicals, many of whom were accused of being Communist agitators. The anti-Communist hysteria of the period has become known as the Red Scare. The wartime suppression of dissent and subsequent Red Scare wounded radical causes in America and led to a weakening of labor unions and near extinction of the Socialist Party.

swelling in her neck, a sign her tuberculosis was back. She took Grant out of boarding school and went to California to rest. During her three months there, she wrote *Woman and the New Race*. The book sounded a lot like *The Woman Rebel*. It claimed that with birth control, women had a duty to not only protect their own freedom to choose motherhood, but to produce superior individuals who could contribute to society. It preached woman's right to enjoy the act of sex. With her manuscript complete, Sanger and Grant returned to New York in May. Sanger continued managing *The Review*, traveled, and promoted birth control.

In 1920, the first year that women could vote, she sailed to England to lecture in Scotland and investigate a German jelly for use with diaphragms. *Woman and the New Race* sold 200,000 copies. In London, Sanger enjoyed herself. Despite their five-year separation, she resumed her intimate friendship with Havelock Ellis. Through mutual friends she was later introduced to the famed author of *War of the Worlds*, H.G. Wells. Taken with Sanger, Wells created "Miss Grammont," a sexually liberated, American birth control supporter in a novel. Their friendship endured for a quarter of a century—despite the intervening Atlantic Ocean and the end of their romantic affair. They corresponded until he died in 1946. (For more information on this famous author, enter "H.G. Wells" into any search engine and browse the sites listed.)

Sanger returned to New York in November 1920, and fell into a slump. Her lectures, by now her only income, were few and far between. Ellis had only reluctantly praised her *Woman and the New Race*. Stung by his coolness, she began work on a new book, *The Pivot of Civilization*. She packed it with statistics, quotes from experts, and documentation that civilization's problems could be solved through limiting family size. Finally, she perked up enough to launch plans for America's first birth control conference to be held in New York City.

The year 1921 was a momentous one for Sanger. On April 5, Sanger met J. Noah H. Slee, who would be her future husband. In May, she returned to Europe, found conference speakers and worked on *Pivot*. A doctor found a pocket of tuberculosis under her tonsils and successfully removed it. Surgery freed her from its twenty-year poisoning of her health. She attended an Amsterdam conference and sailed home to complete her conference arrangements. The event made her the undisputed leader of the birth control movement.

Her conference sponsors included the young Winston Churchill, the secretary of state and eventual prime minister of England, and American novelist Theodore Dreiser. The featured speaker was Harold Cox, former member of the British Parliament. Before the conference, Sanger sent a survey to 31,000 women. The 5,000 who responded proved women were very interested in birth control. The day before the conference, Sanger's socialite friends formed a second group, the American Birth Control League, and named Sanger as president. Physicians, scientists, and birth control advocates on both sides of the Atlantic attended the American Birth Control Conference in New York City. This conference was to end with a discussion at Town Hall. About 30 minutes before Sanger and Cox arrived, however, the police and Monsignor Dineen, secretary to Archbishop Patrick J. Hayes, ordered the meeting stopped. The monsignor told Sanger's assistant, "An indecent, immoral subject is to be discussed."[112] Sanger, Cox, and Sanger's close friend Juliet Rublee found the street jammed. They thought the forum had drawn an overflow audience. Then they realized the police had locked the doors, preventing the crowd from entering. A policeman told her, "You can't get into this place tonight . . . . There ain't going to be no meeting."[113] "But who stopped it?" Sanger asked. "We're the speakers!"[114] Running across the street, Sanger phoned police headquarters. She was told the police had no orders to stop the meeting. No one would tell her how to reach the police commissioner or the mayor. Noticing people exiting a side door, Sanger slipped past the policeman inside.

The auditorium, with spectators, police and clergy, was chaos. Sanger immediately took charge. She later recalled, "I fairly flew up the aisle but halted in front of the footlights; they were as high as my head and another blue uniform was obstructing the steps leading to the stage. Suddenly Lothrop Stoddard, the author, tall and strong, seized me and literally tossed me up to the platform."[115] Shoving the after-speech bouquet of flowers in her hands, he shouted, "Here she is. Here's Mrs. Sanger."[116] On stage, she attempted to take the podium. Spectators cried, "Defy them. Defy them."[117]

She called for silence and then said sarcastically, "One would certainly suppose that this display of liberty and freedom of speech was in Germany, not in America."[118] She got no further. Two policemen, under orders of Police Captain Thomas Donahue, approached her. "They don't dare arrest you," a spectator called. "Where's the warrant? What is the charge?"[119] Sanger tried to speak again. When the policemen grabbed her by the arms, members of the audience jumped on stage to push the police away. She tried unsuccessfully to speak another eight times.

Sanger later wrote, "I knew that I had to keep on [trying to speak] until I was arrested in order that free speech might be made the issue."[120] Others also tried unsuccessfully to speak. The bedlam continued for over an hour until Sanger and members of the American Birth Control League's council were arrested for "disorderly" conduct. The crowd outside was furious. More than 100 policemen were called to maintain order. As Sanger and cohorts walked to jail, a huge crowd of spectators marched behind them, jeering at the police, and singing "My Country 'Tis of Thee."

Every major New York City newspaper, whether they supported birth control or not, ran editorials denouncing the police's violation of free speech. The incident made news all across the country. Then newspaper reporters discovered that Archbishop Hayes had ordered the meeting closed. That the Catholic Church had enough power to control the police angered people across the nation. Monsignor Dineen said the meeting had been closed because of four "growing children," who were actually short-haired college students, in the audience. He acknowledged that he and the Archbishop were "delighted" by the police action because "it was no meeting to be held publicly and without restrictions."[121]

Five days later, on November 18, the forum that started the riot finally took place. Interest was so heightened by the publicity that 1,700 people filled the theater, and 4,000 more tried to get in. Some climbed up fire escapes and looked through windows. Cox lectured, and a play was performed. Sanger spoke eloquently for 10 minutes. She was interrupted with applause numerous times. She attacked the Catholic Church's position that higher education, the right to vote, and knowing about birth control would lower women's morals. She called for a change in the laws that forbade giving contraceptive information to women and asked for the support of physicians. She repeated the movement's principles:

> . . . Birth Control should be available to every adult man and woman. . . We claim that a woman should have the right over her own body and to say if she shall or if she shall not be a mother, as she sees fit. We further claim that the first right of a child is to be desired . . . the second right is that it should be conceived in love, and the third, that it should have a heritage of sound health.[122]

Between the conference and the hearings that investigated the police action in December, the newspapers printed what came to be a war of words between Sanger and the Archbishop. The Archbishop said he had acted for thousands of distressed mothers, "who are alarmed at the daring of the advocates of birth control in bringing out in the open, unrestricted, free

meeting of a subject that simple prudence and decency . . .
should keep within the walls of a clinic."[123] Defending large
families, he pointed out that Benjamin Franklin was the
15th and John Wesley the 18th child in their respective
families. Sanger promptly replied that the Biblical figures of
Isaac, Samuel, and John the Baptist were only children. The
Archbishop issued a Christmas message to his 300 churches.
He called birth control "satanic" and an "unclean abomina-
tion." "Children troop down from heaven because God wills
it,"[124] he said. Sanger declined to debate theory and theology
with him. She said that some, trying to benefit humanity,
"believe that a healthy, happy human race is more in keeping with the laws of God than disease, misery, and poverty
perpetuating themselves."[125]

The investigation of the incident moved beyond Sanger.
Prosecutors arrested Julia Rublee on the witness stand for
saying she read Section 1142 (which prohibited distributing
contraceptive information). She admitted that she knew her
activities broke the law. Rublee was a prominent socialite whose
millionaire husband was a powerful lawyer. His important
friends demanded the mayor investigate the investigation.

The second inquiry to investigate the first inquiry
turned into a circus. The police captain admitted under
oath to taking orders from the telephone operator. He
could not name any superior officer who had directed him
to act. The prosecutors tried to divert attention from the
Town Hall incident to Sanger's beliefs on birth control.
They used her friendships with "subversives" to discredit
her. Sanger, cool under questioning, admitted knowing
radical labor leaders, including Emma Goldman. But she
struck back saying, "I also know Mrs. Andrew Carnegie and
Mr. John D. Rockefeller, Jr. My social relations are with
people of varying ideas and opinions."[126]

In the end, while ridiculed for his evasive answers,
Captain Donahue received no punishment. The controversy

filled the newspapers, however, giving Sanger months of free publicity. Those who had once been Sanger's opponents began to see the injustice of the police and the position of the Catholic Church and began to support her. She abandoned her image as a "radical rebel rouser" and embraced society's inner circle of the respectable.

The controversy increased Sanger's demand as a lecturer, and with increased demand came increased fees. Instead of $50 dollars and expenses, she received $150 to $1,000 for a speech. After years of poverty, Sanger suddenly had a steady, adequate income and growing stature.

The Rebel
Organizes

7

J. Noah Slee met Margaret Sanger on April 1921. Taken by her gaiety, he blurted, "But you cannot be The Margaret Sanger! You don't look like much of a fighter or a lawbreaker."[127] Like Bill Sanger before him, Slee pursued Sanger from the moment he met her. He learned to dance and sent her roses every day. He attended her lectures. He was in the second row at the birth control conference riot.

Slee was an unlikely husband for Sanger. He had been an Episcopal Sunday school superintendent for 25 years. He was not particularly witty, charming, or polished like her British friends. He was a 60-year-old businessman, the president of Three-in-One Oil Company. "What do I want with a man like that?" Sanger asked her secretary. "I don't want to marry anyone, particularly a stodgy churchgoer who isn't interested in art or anything. Yet . . . how often am I going to meet a man with nine million dollars?"[128]

Sanger's divorce from Bill was final in October 1921. By December, Sanger had moved out of her cheap apartment and into the more respectable Gramercy Park area of New York City. Slee's apartment was next to hers. Sanger repeatedly turned down Slee's proposals, explaining she couldn't give up birth control. "Do you want to marry me and spend your honeymoon in the railroad station kissing me good-bye?"[129] she asked. Undaunted, Slee chased her all the more, buying her new office equipment and reorganizing her office's inefficient mail department.

In the summer of 1921, a liberal Japanese organization invited Sanger to lecture on population and war. Thinking Japan was more enlightened than the United States, she accepted. Sanger had long believed that overpopulation would lead to war. Japan seemed ripe for it. In Japan, 2,400 lived in one square mile of agricultural land; in England, the number was 466. But the Japanese government, aware of Sanger's ability to inspire controversy, did not want Sanger. Arriving in San Francisco with 13-year-old Grant and Slee, she found that she had been denied a Japanese visa. Without a visa, she couldn't get a boat ticket.

"I remembered that I had overcome greater obstacles than this one," Sanger later wrote. "My Irish blood was up. I would not take this autocratic 'no' as the final answer."[130] Sanger got her ticket by obtaining it with a visa from China, the ship's next stop after Japan. On the boat, her conversations with the 150 Japanese aboard, they cabled ahead their endorsements.

Arriving in Yokohama, Japan, on March 10, 1922, Sanger was met by government officials, police, and 70 newsmen. After agreeing not to speak specifically about birth control techniques, Sanger entered the country. "They must have thought I possessed some magic wand to depopulate Japan,"[131] she said, after officials confiscated her books. Beyond the government officials, however, Sanger found Japanese people warm and welcoming. She began a lifelong friendship with them, and gave more than 500 speeches and interviews in her month's visit.

"She appeared like a comet," said Baroness Ishimoto, an early supporter of birth control in Japan, "there is no possibility of reckoning the true value of her visit."[132] After Japan, Sanger sailed to Korea. She didn't believe Korean women were ready to fight for their rights. During a speech, her interpreter, embarrassed by Sanger's technical instructions on contraception, asked to be replaced by a doctor. In China, Sanger saw extreme poverty in Peking and Shanghai. She told friends that the millions of starving Chinese "were the best argument in the world for birth control."[133] She went on to Hong Kong, Singapore, and Ceylon. The legacy of her visit included the introduction of three new birth control clinics in Japan and two in China, and a growing international reputation.

Slee prevailed in his pursuit of Sanger, and they were married on September 18, 1922, before a justice of the peace in London. Sanger wore green silk and jade for the wedding. Fearful of scandal, she told only close friends and family the secret. The press discovered it 18 months later. Sanger later admitted, "I made it terribly hard for him. I threw every obstacle in his path."[134] Sanger insisted Slee sign a prenuptial agreement. Included in the agreement were clauses stating that she would keep the Sanger name and live in a separate apartment in their home, and that Slee would never question where she was or with whom. He signed on the dotted line. He always said that Margaret was "the greatest adventure of my life."[135]

The marriage between Sanger and Slee lasted for 21 years. But Slee's "adventure" had its price. He quickly discovered the pattern of their marriage. Sanger frequently went her own way. They celebrated their first and second anniversaries apart. Slee wasn't literary or intellectual like Sanger's British friends. He certainly was not romantic. He once wrote his "angel of love"[136] to bring an enema tube the next time they met or told her how many times he cleaned his teeth.

Slee's most appealing quality appeared to be the money he spent on his "Margy." His gifts included an ermine coat and jewelry. He built her Willowlake, a castle-size country estate that she decorated in red brocades, blue satins, and Chinese rugs. He financed Stuart's and Grant's education. He contributed generously to the American Birth Control League and paid off the debt of *The Birth Control Review*. He financed Sanger's conferences. He later smuggled diaphragms into the United States through his oil company and produced a German-formula spermicide in one of his factories. He asked for contributions from his wealthy friends. In return for his financial support, Sanger was very grateful.

The American Birth Control League received thousands of letters from women pleading for contraceptive information. Sanger's staff returned each letter with a copy of *Family Limitation*, which recommended use of a diaphragm. But some women couldn't pay a doctor to fit them with one. To help women like these, Sanger organized the Birth Control Clinical Research Bureau. The Bureau, staffed with a physician, could legally give out contraceptive information for the prevention and cure of disease. Besides helping poor women, Sanger also wanted to gather statistics on contraceptive use. After fitting each patient with a diaphragm, Sanger wanted a case history, a check-up two to three days after the fitting, another check-up three months later, and a final check-up in a year for each patient.

The Birth Control Clinical Research Bureau (calling it a clinic would have required a special license) was located across the hall from Sanger's American Birth Control League. The Bureau did not advertise. Its presence spread by word-of-mouth and did not reject any woman who could not pay. Sanger opened the Bureau on January 1, 1923, but two years of precious data was discounted by the medical community because the Bureau's first physician kept incomplete records. Sanger replaced her with Dr. Hannah Stone. After joining its staff, Stone was asked to resign from the hospital where she worked because of birth control's controversial nature and for years was denied membership in the New York Academy of Medicine. Still, she volunteered to work without pay for the Bureau. During her first year, Stone prescribed contraception for 1,600 women. She kept meticulous records (100,000 over her entire career). At the Sixth International Neo-Malthusian and Birth Control Conference in 1925, over 1,000 physicians heard Stone's findings on the diaphragm's success. She later published some of the first contraceptive studies in medical journals.

The 1925 conference brought delegates from 18 countries to New York City. In a breakthrough, a member of the Medical Association spoke out for birth control for the first time. By conference end, the first international birth control organization was organized, with Sanger as president.

Sanger planned another conference, the Geneva Population Conference, for August 31, 1927. It was a mammoth undertaking. She flitted around Europe, mostly without Slee, planning for the Swiss gathering. She brought in scientists and

Eugenics

During the 1920s, Margaret Sanger expanded support for birth control by promoting it on the basis of medical and public health needs. In 1921 she embarked on a campaign of education and publicity designed to win the public's support for birth control by founding the American Birth Control League. She focused many of her efforts on gaining support from the medical profession and social workers, and at times her thought overlapped with that of the more liberal wing of the movement called eugenics. **Eugenics** is the science of improving hereditary qualities by controlling the means of human reproduction. Eugenicists believe that people with good genes should be encouraged to reproduce, and that people with bad genes should be discouraged from reproducing.

Like the eugenicists, Sanger rationalized the use of birth control as a means of reducing hereditary (inherited) mental or physical defects. She at times agreed with those who supported sterilization for the mentally incompetent. However, there continues to be controversy over the degree to which she agreed with the movement as a whole. One important difference is that Sanger believed that the individual and not the state should make reproductive decisions, as the following quote from *The Birth Control Review* illustrates:

Eugenists imply or insist that a woman's first duty is to the state; we contend that her duty to herself is her first duty to the state. We maintain that a woman possessing an adequate knowledge of her reproductive functions is the best judge of the time and conditions under which her child should be brought into the world.*

* Margaret Sanger, "Birth Control and Racial Betterment," *The Birth Control Review* 3(1919): 11–12. Reprinted in *The Birth Control Review Vol. I, Vols. 1–3, 1917–1919* (New York: Da Capo Press, 1970).

academics from around the world to study population growth, funding the gathering with grants from J. D. Rockefeller, other wealthy benefactors, and, of course, Slee.

Leery of Sanger's celebrity, the delegates did not want their colleagues back home to know a woman had organized the conference. Sanger agreed not to lead any discussions and reluctantly agreed to remove the names of the women volunteers from the program. By the end of the conference, the delegates had been charmed by her sincerity and gave her a standing ovation.

Slee was troubled by the amount of time he spent alone and by the on-again-off-again nature of the marriage. Sanger acknowledged his unhappiness, while trying to justify her absences to him. Sending him off to London alone after the Geneva Conference, she wrote, "My heart is troubled to have you lonely and apart from life's activities but I should wither up and die to be shut off from the intellectual currents of my contemporaries."[137] In October 1927, Sanger and Slee traveled to Switzerland. Slee loved their luxurious vacation, while Sanger complained to her sons, "I am no good as a loafer."[138] The more time she spent with Slee, the less she liked him. She wrote a friend, "He will not let me out of his sight without a protest. I feel sorry for him and yet can I go on like this?"[139]

A shock awaited Sanger on their return to New York. The American Birth Control League's Board of Directors wanted Sanger to have less control of the organization. They thought that the days of banner waving and headline grabbing were past and that the organization should grow slowly and methodically. The directors took over much of Sanger's power to the point that she could not spend money without their authorization. Fed up, Sanger resigned as president on June 12, 1928. Later she wrote, "I was always willing to present my facts to experts and abide by their superior knowledge. . . . But I was no paper president . . . and I could not well observe the dictates of people who did not know my subject as well as I did."[140] The Board that controlled the American Birth Control League and *The Birth Control Review* underestimated Sanger's importance to the organization. Along with Sanger, J. Noah Slee resigned as the League's treasurer and chief benefactor. Over four years, he had donated $64,000 to his wife's cause. The League was never financially sound again.

Sanger, however, refused to give up control of the Birth Control Clinical Research Bureau. She said, "I felt it was my responsibility, and belonged to me personally."[141] By the time the police raided it on April 15, 1929, it was a well-established service in the community. The staff included doctors, part-time doctors, nurses, social workers, and volunteers. With new patients and repeat and follow-up clients, it helped more women than the combined efforts of all the other birth control clinics throughout the country. For six years, the Bureau had peacefully helped women with contraception and gathered statistics on birth control.

Then, as in the Brownsville Clinic raid, an undercover police-woman visited the Bureau. Weeks later, eight policemen burst into the Bureau's offices. Under Policewoman Mary Sullivan's orders, fifteen patients were taken outside and forced to give their names. The policemen arrested two physicians and six staff members for violating the Comstock law. Dr. Hannah Stone thought the situation ironic. She later told Sanger, "Only a few moments ago a visiting physician from the Middle West asked one of the nurses whether we ever had any police interference. 'Oh, no', the nurse cheerfully replied, 'Those days are over.'"[142]

Along with arrests, the police confiscated the medical records from the Bureau. While birth control supporters had been arrested before, this was the first time that police had seized confidential medical records. Sanger, 50 years old and now well experienced in confrontations, put up a good fight.

"You have no right to touch those files," she told Mrs. Sullivan. "Not even the nurses ever see them. They are the private property of the doctors; and if you take them you will get into trouble."

"Trouble," Sullivan responded. "I get into trouble? What about the trouble you're in?"

"I wouldn't change mine for yours," Sanger retorted.

"Well, this is my party," said Sullivan. "You keep out."[143]

Of course, Sanger would do no such thing. She accompanied her staff to the police station, where they were booked and then released on $300 bail. Birth control was back in the news. Doctors, whose support Sanger so wanted, backed her and the right of doctor-patient privilege. Both the New York County Medical Society and the New York Academy of Medicine protested the police action.

A month after the hearing on April 21, the charges against Sanger and the staff were dropped for lack of evidence and the medical records were returned. Just as in the Town Hall riot, the publicity the police caused was better than anything birth control could have planned. So many women showed up after the raid that the Bureau had to increase both its office hours and the days it was open. (In an ironic twist, Anna McNamara, the policewoman decoy, visited the Bureau subsequently for treatment of several serious medical conditions that had been discovered during her undercover visit, each of which qualified her to receive a diaphragm.)

After the raid, Sanger wondered why the police raided such a helpful little agency "which was functioning quietly and successfully in an obscure side street, minding its own business, and hoping that its powerful ecclesiastical neighbors might mind theirs."[144] She already knew the answer to her question. The police acted because of the Catholic Church's influence in the city. The Bureau had operated so quietly that the Church hierarchy didn't know it existed until women asked Catholic social workers where the Bureau was located.

The medical community might have embraced the Bureau sooner had Sanger surrendered the Bureau's leadership to a committee of male physicians or even become affiliated with committees or hospitals that were part of the medical establishment. But Sanger knew the Bureau's reputation for caring came from its female staff and administrators. Like the poor women she had once treated, female patients were more comfortable confiding their silent fears and whispered questions to other women.

In October 1929, the stock market crashed, sending the price of stock plummeting and ushering in the Great Depression of the 1930s. Remarkably, the Bureau was scarcely affected by the Great Depression. Sanger's contacts with the Rockefellers, J.P. Morgan, and, of course, J. Noah Slee kept it afloat. In 1930, Slee purchased a new building for it and personally carried its mortgage. Through it all, the Bureau's secret weapon was Margaret Sanger. She was a tireless in her support and fundraising for her clinic.

The Rebel
and the Law

8

Whether universally accepted or not, birth control was no longer confined to the "back alleys" of people's minds. A second generation of supporters joined the movement, many of whom were unaware of its past. One new member to the American Birth Control League urged Sanger to join the campaign to support birth control clinics. Sanger, appalled at the newcomer's lack of history replied, "When were you born?"[145] Believing she had significant public support behind her, Sanger next set her sights on Congress. In August 1929, she formed the National Committee for Federal Legislation on Birth Control. Her goal was to replace the old Comstock laws with a new "doctor's bill, " one that would allow physicians to give out contraceptive advice for any reason and to use the mail, if necessary, to do it.

Sanger hoped there would be strength in numbers. She set about creating a network of volunteers all over the country. She started small, gathering supporters in each Congressional District and then branching out to the state and regional levels. She enlisted people who had worked on women's **suffrage**, the movement to secure voting rights for women. Sanger lobbied prominent, civic-minded matrons who had access to enormous wealth. She persuaded some organizations that were afraid to be linked publicly with birth control to make anonymous donations. She approached Protestant groups and national women's organization for support. Sanger wrote to women all over the country, to make them aware of laws "that condemn us to conditions our Government would not impose upon a farmer's cattle,"[146] and encouraged them to write their Congressmen. She included a self-addressed and stamped envelope for them to use.

Sponsoring a bill about anything so controversial as contraception was political suicide. With an eye on the power-ful Catholic Church, many congressmen declined to become involved. One told National Committee volunteers, "It is revolting to interfere in people's personal affairs." Another said

Mary Ware Dennett

Mary Ware Dennett (1872–1947) was a contemporary of Margaret Sanger who worked mainly in competition with rather than in cooperation with Sanger. While an important organizer in the suffrage movement, Dennett is best known for her work in birth control and sex education. In 1915, when William Sanger was arrested, Dennett attended several meetings and was attracted to the movement for contraceptive freedom. While Margaret Sanger was in exile abroad, Dennett organized the National Birth Control League (NBCL), the first organization in the country founded to legalize contraception. While Dennett strongly believed in fighting for birth control through legal channels, Sanger believed in civil disobedience, such as the establishment of birth control clinics. When Margaret Sanger approached the NBCL in 1916 for support for her Brownsville Clinic, she was denied. A rivalry between the two women began that was to last for years.

The NBCL later disbanded, and Dennett formed a new organization, the Voluntary Parenthood League (VPL), to carry on her efforts. The sole aim of the VPL was repeal of the Comstock Act through legislation that would delete the phrase "for the prevention of contraception" from the law, thereby permitting the free dissemination of information about birth control. In Dennett's view, this "open bill" would guarantee all women access to contraceptive information and devices, even those who could not afford a physician. Sanger argued that the "open bill" would flood the mails with unscientific and unreliable information. She chose to focus on a "doctor's bill" that gave the medical establishment control of the distribution of birth control information and devices. The differences between Sanger and Dennett set the stage for a competitive and at times confrontational relationship that some feel hurt the movement.

he didn't think "there would be any virtue among women if such a law were passed." [147]

Sanger then approached congressmen whose terms were ending. In 1931 she asked Frederick Gillette, a 79-year-old senator from Massachusetts. Near retirement, he was not worried about alienating any of his Catholic constituents. With his sponsorship, Sanger gathered experts in religion, economics, and physicians, to speak for the bill in the hearings. She read a list of supporters to the committee members. "I still cannot believe this is *the* Mrs. Sanger," wrote a reporter of her simple dress, curly hair, and "wistful" face. "How anyone could bear to commit her to jail for even an hour I can't imagine."[148]

The Catholic Church gathered its own experts. One argued that the bill would open a "floodgate" of pornographic literature.[149] Another opponent testified that birth control was a Russian plot to ruin America. One argued that great men, many of whom were born poor, used poverty to "fire them with ambition."[150]

Sanger looked cool and composed during the opposition's testimony. She later recalled that "the inward fury that possessed me warmed from coldness to white heat." [151] With only 10 minutes to respond, she reminded the Committee that this birth control movement started in America, not in Russia. She pointed out only one-sixth of 120 million Americans were Catholic. She argued the rest of the country should be able to decide about birth control themselves. Never one to mince words, she disagreed that great leaders came from large families. She said, "I would like to call to your attention that the great leader of Christianity, Jesus Christ himself, was said to be an only child."[152] Catholics in the audience gasped and crossed themselves.

The bill died in committee. The deciding vote was cast by a senator who hadn't even attended the hearings.

Sanger started her campaign over again and used every opportunity to advance her cause. In November 1931,

American Woman's Association chose Sanger for its first Annual Gold Medal as "outstanding woman in the metropolitan area" for her "vision, integrity, and valor."[153] At the dinner on April 20, 1932, Sanger was charming and witty. Accepting the honor she said, "For after nearly twenty years of indictment, suppressions, courts, jails, patrol wagons and police raids, it is simply wonderful . . . to receive something besides a warrant."[154] Then she summarized her congressional campaign. She told of competing with **Prohibition**, unemployment, and the budget for attention. She described the struggle with her archenemy, the Catholic Church.

In 1932, Senator Henry Hatfield of West Virginia sponsored a second bill. He negotiated privately between Sanger and National Catholic Welfare Conference representatives to reword the bill so that both sides could accept it. His efforts failed. To counter the growing influence of Sanger's national campaign, the opposition included powerful testimony by the National Council of Catholic Women and the Knights of Columbus. A popular radio host, Father Charles E. Coughlin, testified against the bill. He asked, "Why are they [contraceptives] around the high schools? To teach them how to fornicate and not get caught. All this bill means is 'How to commit adultery and not get caught'."[155] Some spectators and members of the subcommittee left the room in disgust. It was the same old argument wrapped in an insult: If women controlled contraception, it would lead to immoral behavior.

There was also a new argument to debate. Some proposed that, because of the Depression, the nation needed more people, not less, to buy things. Sanger called those who supported that idea "boneheads, spineless and brainless."[156] To her, the more people who were on public relief, the higher taxes would rise to support them. Despite her efforts, the bill, sponsored by Senator Hatfield, died in committee.

Sanger paid the price for her constant lobbying and lecturing. She suffered from severe stomach pains and terrible headaches. The 52-year-old Sanger was undaunted, though. She wrote Havelock Ellis, "Next time we will win!"[157] Her frequent absences still troubled Slee. During the legislative sessions, Slee stayed with Sanger in Washington. But shortly after, they went their separate ways. Sanger insisted on traveling, working on birth control, and shuttling back and forth to England instead of being at Slee's side.

In 1933, an argument nearly ended their marriage. Exhausted from Congressional hearings, Sanger asked Slee to book a Bermuda vacation. His response came back like a shot. Years later, Sanger recalled in an interview that he yelled over the phone, "She was wasting her life on a cause no one cared about, except a bunch of nuts. She should take her vacation alone and not bother to come back!"[158] After calming down, Slee arranged the Bermuda trip, expecting Sanger to appear at the dock. When she did not, he went on alone, while Sanger and a friend vacationed in the Bahamas. The couple returned to Willowlake at about the same time. Slee greeted her with "Hello darling, did you have a good time?"[159] Although Sanger was prepared to leave him right then, they made up over champagne.

The couple continued on just as they had. Sanger continued to engage in relationships outside the marriage. Her affair with Angus Sneed MacDonald, a businessman, lasted two years. He sent flowers, champagne, and love letters to Willowlake right under the nose of Slee. Though MacDonald wanted her to marry him, Sanger would not risk harming the movement if she divorced for a second time. "I still want to fly or climb difficult heights and be moving onward and upwards toward the unknown," she said told him. "I'm not a peaceful or restful person to know at all."[160]

In 1934, a third version of "the doctor's bill" nearly passed. The National Committee for Federal Legislation on Birth Control had sponsored over 800 lectures through the country to gain support. The Catholic Church increased its negative campaign, publishing its position in magazine and newspaper editorials. It continually urged its supporters to write their congressmen. Because of the Catholic Church's vicious opposition, Sanger expected yet one more defeat. Surprisingly, the Senate Judiciary Committee sent the bill to the Senate floor. Achieving that was a tremendous victory for birth control.

Ironically, vote on "the doctor's bill" was scheduled on the session's last day, just like the Comstock law long ago. Birth control supporters hoped it would slip through by voice vote among the 200 other bills on the docket. On June 13, 1934, it was read three times, voted on, and passed. But just as the birth control representatives celebrated, a Catholic senator asked that the bill be recalled. By voice vote, the senators politely obliged. Referred back to committee, the bill again died.

The "doctor's bill" made millions more aware of birth control. National organizations, like the Council of Jewish women, General Federation of Women's Clubs, and the Young Women's Christian Association (YWCA) endorsed it. But neither Margaret Sanger's grit nor six years of work by thousands of volunteers could repeal the Comstock Laws.

In the meantime, Sanger stepped up her travels to promote birth control on an international level. On July 3, 1935, Sanger and Grant visited Russia. At 77 years old, Slee was not up to the trip. It proved an unpleasant journey for Sanger. The cold Russian summer aggravated the arthritis in her legs, and she was ill with vomiting and diarrhea. She had come to see a famous Russian birth control program and investigate a new spermicide. But the Russian program consisted of aborting pregnancies rather than preventing them. Women received a six-minute abortion, without anesthesia, for about $2.50. The Russian women said they knew nothing of birth control.

Sanger was invited to speak during the All-India Woman's Conference from December 28, 1935, to January 2, 1936. Its previous conference had endorsed birth control, but the 1935 organizers wanted Sanger to "put teeth in it"[161] with a concrete plan for India. Sanger planned a three-month tour. She brought her own publicist to write articles for Indian newspapers and to keep birth control in the news back in the United States. She started in London at a fundraising dinner with H.G. Wells, and she met Jawaharal Nehru, Mahatma Gandhi's designated successor.

When she landed in Bombay, she was greeted with garlands of flowers and large crowds. A country teeming with people, India had recorded a 370 million population only four years before. With an increase of 10 percent per decade, India added 1,027 births per day. However, infant death rates were equally horrible. One half of all Indian children died before 5 years of age.

In a country with the second-largest population in the world after China, Sanger found her constant enemy. At the All-India Women's Conference, Catholic supporters convinced the local rulers that birth control would lead to promiscuity and **racial suicide**, the belief that a low birth rate would lead to the extinction of a particular race of people. Sanger was instructed to discuss only prostitution, something less controversial, and avoid birth control directly. Sanger politely and briefly addressed prostitution before the group, but then went right into birth control.

In India, Sanger traveled over 10,000 miles. She spoke at many meetings, broadcast over Bombay radio, and generated newspaper articles for the benefit of Congress, back in the United States, that was considering "the doctor's bill." She snagged an endorsement of a national medical association and established contacts between interested Indians and a supplier of a foam powder contraceptive. She gave demonstrations on contraceptives. Her talks among the middle class led to the establishment of 20 birth control clinics in India.

The highlight of her trip was meeting with Mahatma Gandhi, India's revered leader of nonviolence. She had hoped

Gandhi would endorse birth control, but quickly realized his mind was already set. He agreed that families should be smaller, no more than three children. He suggested couples should only have intercourse three or four times during their marriage. If men could not contain themselves, Gandhi suggested a woman should "resist"[162] her husband's advances and leave him if necessary. Both suggestions, in any country, were impossible. He did think that the rhythm method might be permissible, but Sanger could not use this concession in her publicity.

Back in the United States, the U.S. Court of Appeals rendered a new interpretation of the Comstock Laws. In 1932, a package of contraceptives mailed from a Japanese physician to Sanger had been seized by the postal authorities. Sanger then asked her Japanese physician to send more contraceptives to Dr. Hannah Stone at the Birth Control Clinical Research Bureau. Sanger then filed suit because the postal authorities had seized a package mailed directly to a physician. The case, *United States* v. *One Package Containing 120 More or Less Rubber Pessaries to Prevent Conception*, was filed on November 10, 1933. It wound its way through the court system for three years.

In December 7, 1936, the United States Circuit Court of Appeals ruled that physicians could send contraceptive literature and devices through the mail. One of the three judges said that the time had passed when birth control items were literally immoral. "In my excitement, I actually fell downstairs," Sanger wrote of the decision. "Here was the culmination of unremitting labor . . . the gratification of a dream come true."[163]

Though Dr. Stone's lawyer called the decision "the end of birth control laws," that wasn't quite true.[164] The Court's decision tore the teeth out of the dragon, but the Comstock law stayed on the books. Thirty-four more years later, in 1970, contraception between married people became legal. Two years later, the unmarried finally got that right.

By 1937, birth control was finally becoming more accepted. After 16 years, Sanger was honored with the New York City Town Hall Club's medal "for contributing to the enlargement and enrichment of life."[165] The American Medical Association grudgingly admitted that contraception and its methods could be taught in medical schools. Sears Roebuck catalogs began advertising contraceptives, and gas stations sold them as "preventatives."

In 1938, Sanger published *Margaret Sanger: An Autobiography.* It was a fuller and more colorful account of her life than her 1931 autobiography, *My Fight for Birth Control.* The new version also included conversations with Slee, her children, the police, her lovers, and international leaders. Part travelogue and part history, the book detailed the many levels of her life. On one page it described the emaciated Japanese rickshaw drivers who carried her from place to place, and on the next it described an elegant society dinner she attended. She wrote about the yellow sand of the Suez Canal, the ochre color of an Indian swami's robes, and the rats that scurried through Indian streets.

The pioneering days of birth control were passing. Ever since the *One Package* decision allowed physicians to prescribe contraceptives and send information through the mail, Sanger widened her focus. In the country's rural areas of the country, the poor couldn't pay for a doctor's contraceptive advice. Sanger argued that if government services included birth control, information would be available to everyone. She targeted the Deep South and migrant camps in California.

To simplify fundraising efforts, she agreed to merge her Bureau with the same American Birth Control League that had once rejected her and had competed with her efforts for years. After long negotiations, in 1939, the two groups merged to become the Birth Control Federation of America, with Sanger named its honorary chairman.

Sanger had moved in 1937 to Tucson, Arizona, a place she had visited earlier in her life and had liked very much. There, no longer at the head of the family planning movement that she founded, she painted, joined the art club, and helped the Tucson Mother's Health Clinic.

9

The Rebel
Slows Down

The Margaret Sanger who thrived on newspaper headlines did not like being Mrs. J. Noah Slee of Tucson, Arizona. She was no longer in the thick of the national family planning movement. Moreover, she was increasingly dissatisfied with life with Slee. She complained that Slee had no outside interests except counting his money and did little but gripe. Sanger judged his dinner conversation to be "trite and stupid."[166]

Sanger's suggestion that the government take responsibility for birth control did not go far. In 1939, a total of 539 birth control centers operated throughout the United States. President Franklin Roosevelt's Intergovernmental Committee to Coordinate Health and Welfare Policy invited Sanger to testify in January 1939. She pointed out that 37 percent of the national income went toward welfare programs and suggested that if funding for birth control was included in government programs, it would "probably do more for the health and happiness of mothers and children than any other single instrument."[168] The suggestion would not go far without President Roosevelt's approval, and the president saw birth control as too hot a topic to champion.

Sanger learned that she could not even count on her close friends for support. She was shattered when Havelock Ellis, her former lover and constant correspondent, died. Yet his autobiography mentioned Sanger only as "M," and revealed "I have sometimes been tempted to wish that I had not met her."[168] His snub cut Sanger to the quick.

Sanger fired up her righteous indignation in October 1940, to battle a Massachusetts law that called contraceptives "Crimes against Chastity, Morality, Decency and Good Order."[169] The Planned Parenthood League of Massachusetts asked Sanger to campaign against it. Over 1,600 people heard her speak in Boston. But in Holyoke, in the western part of the state, the Catholic Church "encouraged" local businesses to cancel her upcoming speech. Crumbling under the threat of a Catholic boycott to their businesses, businessmen called off the lecture. Nearby communities invited her, but Sanger declined. "No," she told them, "I will accept none, I will speak *here*."[170] Her determination was vintage Sanger. Just two hours before the speech, a local union offered its meeting rooms, where Sanger spoke eloquently to 70 people. Two years later, the repeal of Massachusetts' "little Comstock law" failed, again after intense Catholic pressure. As added insult, the Boston libraries branded Sanger's autobiography as obscene.

The following years brought new pleasures into her life. The hole left by her own beloved daughter's death was partially filled by the birth of two granddaughters. In November, Margaret Sanger II was born to Stuart and his wife. Nineteen months later, Barbara Nancy arrived.

On January 29, 1942 the Birth Control Federation of America was renamed Planned Parenthood Federation of America. Times were changing. The name symbolized a shift to a less controversial philosophy. Sanger, the mother of the movement, watched from the sidelines in Tucson, where she increasingly devoted herself to tending her ailing husband. A series of strokes in Tucson and in Willowlake had left Slee nearly paralyzed, and Sanger gave up all activities, including writing, to tend to him. On June 21, 1943, Slee died in his sleep. Grant and Stuart paid their respects, but none of his children or grandchildren attended the services. Money smart to the end, Slee left his "Margy" a $5,000,000 bank account.

In her late 60s and on her own, Sanger took up cooking, and held elaborate dinner parties. Guests ate Japanese food sitting on the floor in their socks. Champagne and laughter overflowed. On one New Year's Eve, her guests telephoned Hitler to give a "Bronx cheer." The plan was working until a German secretary on the other end realized the call was a joke. Stuart's family dined with her every Thursday. Her granddaughters helped her, playing "dress up" in clothing that Sanger had collected from her travels.

At 66, Sanger also learned to drive a car. As in her life, Sanger paid little attention to any obstacles in her way, driving about town in a large hat and white gloves. Though her friends were horrified at the 21-year age difference, she began a relationship with Hobson Pittman, a landscape painter in Tucson. Pittman liked her "exuberant gaiety."[171] The relationship lasted six years. Sanger wrote a friend that he was fun, but "not for keeps."[172]

Even in retirement, Sanger kept speaking out on and thinking about birth control. Touring family planning clinics across the country, Sanger realized that the diaphragm was not a perfect form of contraception. Poor women needed a simpler and cheaper form of birth control, something like a "birth control pill."[173] She approached Planned Parenthood for funding for the idea. Strapped for money just to survive, the organization declined her request.

Tucking the idea away for another time, Sanger turned to the international scene. In August 1946, she addressed a family planning conference in Stockholm, Sweden. The delegates wanted to create a permanent international family planning organization. Despite her frail health, Sanger went to work, finding a place for the next conference, pledging $5,000 of her own money for expenses. She snagged grants from the prestigious Rockefeller family and a close friend, Mrs. Stanley McCormick, whose biggest contribution to birth control was yet to come.

Two years later, in January 1948, the Cheltenham Conference on Population and World Resources in Relation to the Family took place in England. Out of it came the International Committee on Planned Parenthood. "Almost single-handed, she created this conference . . . out of nothing but will power," said a friend, who added at the same time, "[she] was unyielding, relentless, and egotistical."[174]

The movement's new leaders realized the increase in the world's population was alarming, but preferred slow and cautious studies. They didn't believe the poor should be helped first, and they certainly didn't believe women could solve a worldwide problem. They were put off by Sanger's intensity. Then, too, members of The Planned Parenthood Federation of America weren't happy with Sanger's leadership of the international movement. They wanted more influence in making decisions in that arena and clashed with Sanger. Arthur Packard, a friend who influenced how the Rockefeller family directed their charitable contributioins, said of Sanger, "Mrs. Sanger is perhaps losing her ability to enlist the cooperation, support and collaboration of key people at the policy level."[175]

Sanger's life was changing. Her husband and many old comrades were gone. The cause did not always welcome her. One bright spot was the Honorary Doctorate of Laws awarded by Smith College on June 6, 1949. Sanger, who collected letters, journals, and newspaper clippings throughout her career, responded by donating many of them to Smith.

Another bright spot was the warm support of the country of Japan. After the war, marriage, birth rates, and the population had soared, increasing by one million every year. The Family Planning Association invited Sanger to Japan. As in her first visit years before, she was denied a visa. This time, General Douglas MacArthur, who headed America's occupation forces in Japan, kept her out. Officials thought that Japan "did not need Margaret Sanger barnstorming in Japan. Birth control has nothing to do with population problems."[176] Sixteen months later, President Harry Truman relieved MacArthur from duty, and the visa was granted. Sanger did not immediately leave for Japan. In August 1949, the 70-year-old Sanger overexerted herself in the Tucson heat and suffered her first attack. Recovering for six weeks in the hospital, she faced her own mortality. She wrote an English friend, "There is no organ of the body that gives one pause like a heart attack. Just one little beat too few & out you go."[177] Though clogged arteries are easily treated today, no such help existed for Sanger. After a second heart attack, she suffered continually from sharp, intense chest pains. They changed her charm into eccentricity, her single-mindedness to shrillness.

Sanger had helped design her new house, a fan-shaped structure with a 40-foot glass view of the Catalina foothills of Tucson. It included a Japanese garden, a desert garden, and a fountain connected to a lily pond in Sanger's front room. She insisted on checking its construction, telling her doctor, "I am rich. I have brains. I shall do exactly as I please."[178] In 1950, Sanger was to receive the Lasker Award of the Planned Parenthood Association in recognition of her pioneering work in family planning. Too weak to go herself, Sanger sent Grant with her acceptance for the award. The October 1950 speech was not one of her best. It attacked welfare programs for not eliminating the "feeble minded and unfit" and proposed "incentive sterilization."[179] Today, **tubal sterilizations**, called ligations (in women), and **vasectomies** (in men) are common. But such recommendations, coming after the atrocities of Nazi Holocaust, where many Jewish and other victims were subjected to forced sterilization, were a grave mistake. Once known for her reasonable presentations, the speech shed a negative light on Sanger. Already discredited with some birth control organizations, she lost face with the new generation of reformers.

In October 1952, Sanger finally sailed from Honolulu for her third Japanese trip. Her family feared the stress of the trip would overwhelm her health, but Sanger pressed on. She hoped to convince Japanese audiences that prevention was better birth control than abortion, which Japanese women used as "after-the-fact" birth control. Sanger was welcomed in Japan like royalty for having brought their country a means to to deal with the problem of overpopulation. Fifty girls in elaborate kimonos formed a reception line for her. She was crowned with a wreath of chrysanthemums while 140 newsmen recorded the event. Loudspeakers, mounted on trucks announced, "Sanger! Sanger!" People crowded around her and tried to kiss her hand. She met with government officials, gave interviews, spoke on radio, and visited birth control clinics. She proposed a new teaching clinic and recommended educational programs and research begin as well. She suggested an alternative to abortion could be training the 20,000 Japanese midwives to instruct couples about contraceptives.

Sanger traveled on to Bombay, India, to address the Third International Conference on Planned Parenthood. For a year, organizing the November event had rested squarely on her tiny shoulders. She invited Indian doctors to the conference and cajoled American doctors to finance their trip. She got friends to become benefactors and even obtained a quote from Albert Einstein. Although he could not pledge money, Prime Minister Nehru endorsed birth control at the conference. That the head of a government supported birth control was astonishing. Sanger brought $2,500 from her Tucson friends to add one more to the 106 existing clinics there.

Back in Tucson, Sanger continued to try to heal herself through yoga and spiritual healing, as well as diet and taking vitamins. She also turned her mind again to finding a cheaper and simpler alternative to the diaphragm. She investigated a German jelly, a Russian spermicide, and herbs from Fiji without success. She thought that perhaps an immunization or a shot would be a better form of contraception.

Gregory Pincus was a researcher at the Worchester Foundation for Experimental Biology. In 1953, Pincus discovered essential elements in developing an **oral contraceptive**, a pill that could be taken to prevent pregnancy. With a modest grant from Planned Parenthood, he had discovered that the hormone **progesterone** stopped ovulation in 90 percent of his cases. Planned Parenthood, however, did not seem interested in his findings. The aging Sanger, despite her health problems, knew an important discovery when she saw one. In June 1953, she brought Kate McCormick and Gregory Pincus together.

Sanger and Kate McCormick had been friends since Sanger's 1917 arrest. They spent summers together in McCormick's Santa Barbara, California, cottage. Sanger enjoyed the climate and mingling with McCormick's wealthy acquaintances. McCormick had helped fund conferences and

The Birth Control Pill

The birth control pill ("the Pill") is a pill that, taken daily, prevents pregnancy. The earliest pills only contained the hormone progesterone, which works by thickening the mucous around the cervix, preventing the sperm from entering the uterus. It also affects the lining of the uterus so if the egg is fertilized, it cannot attach to the wall of the uterus. Most birth control pills now contain a combination of the hormones estrogen and progesterone to prevent ovulation, the release of an egg during the monthly cycle. If a woman doesn't ovulate, she cannot get pregnant because there is no egg to be fertilized.

The combination pill comes in either a 21-day pack or a 28-day pack. One hormone pill is taken each day at about the same time for 21 days. Depending on the pack, a woman will stop taking pills for 7 days or she will take a reminder pill that contains no hormones for 7 days. A woman has her period after she stops taking the pills with hormones.

Over the course of one year, about 5 out of 100 typical couples who rely on the Pill to prevent pregnancy will have an accidental pregnancy, giving it a 95 percent efficiency. The Pill is an effective form of birth control, but it does not protect against sexually transmitted diseases (STDs). For those having sex, condoms must always be used along with birth control pills to protect against STDs. It also has some side effects, which can include nausea, weight gain, headaches, dizziness, breast tenderness, mood changes, and a tendency to form blood clots. A doctor or a nurse practitioner must prescribe the pill.

the Clinical Research Bureau. She had even smuggled diaphragms into the country for the Bureau. With a degree in biology from the Massachusetts Institute of Technology, she was no mere society matron.

Sanger asked McCormick to help fund the research on oral contraceptives. The commitment was not as simple as writing a number on a check. It was a long-term, open-ended project, requiring large sums of money. In all, McCormick would contribute $2,000,000 towards "the Pill," and left another $1,000,000 to the project in her will. "Had not Mrs. McCormick come to our rescue financially," a Worchester Foundation director wrote 16 years later, "the pill would not have been developed. It was a direct growth of her financial aid."[180] The formidable Mrs. McCormick, however, would likely never have stepped in except for the lobbying of Sanger. In October 1955, Pincus announced arrival of "the Pill." Pincus later simply said, "I invented The Pill at the request of a woman."[181] He was referring to Margaret Sanger.

As her health permitted, Sanger stayed on the road. At the Fourth International Planned Parenthood Federation conference in Sweden, Sanger was elected president of the International Planned Parenthood Federation. Her responsibilities would keep her moving, including more trips to Japan. In 1954 Sanger appeared on the radio broadcast "This I Believe," hosted by the legendary reporter Edward R. Murrow. In that Monday night broadcast, Sanger summed up her life's work. She said, "I believed it was my duty to place motherhood on a higher level than enslavement and accident . . . . No matter what it may cost in health, in misunderstanding, in sacrifice, something had to be done, and I felt that I was called by the force of circumstances to do it."[182]

An astonishing number of people, some 39 million in America alone, heard the daughter of an Irish immigrant speak that night. It was one of the last shining moments of a remarkable woman's life.

Rebel of
the Century

10

The last dozen years of Sanger's life turned into a slow unraveling of the mind, body, and power of an extraordinary woman. Sanger's third trip to Japan both honored and betrayed her deteriorating condition. In April 4, 1954, the International Planned Parenthood Federation sent her to participate in the first national meeting of the Japan Federation of Family Planning and to invite it into the international organization. She helped organize the 1955 conference (where Pincus would talk about "the Pill"). She met the Japanese emperor and spoke before the Japanese national legislature. She told its members "birth control could eventually solve the vital Japanese problem of overpopulation."[183] This event was an honor never before given to a foreign woman. But her health and mind simply could not produce the clear and insightful suggestions of the past, and sometimes her speeches wandered.

Back in the United States, Sanger tried to stay active in the International Planned Parenthood Federation. She was still able to collect small donations from her many wealthy friends. Few listened to her proposals. Sensing new leaders, and perhaps fearful of being replaced, she unfairly criticized the Federation's suggestions. Even her close friend Dorothy Brush called her "bitchy, ruthless and cruel"[184] But no one dared suggest that the famous standard bearer step aside.

Television's glaring lights exposed Sanger's mental and physical frailties to the nation. She accepted reporter Mike Wallace's invitation to appear on his 30-minute television program for a philosophical discussion of birth control. Instead, during the September 21, 1957 interview, Wallace attacked Sanger personally. He accused her of leaving her family. He asked if she believed in God? He asked what were her personal views on infidelity and divorce. He even brought out the timeworn question: Wouldn't birth control destroy the morals of a nation?

The Margaret Sanger who defied entire governments and powerful institutions once could have battled Wallace word for word. But a befuddled, aging Sanger was not prepared to answer these attacks on her personal life and personal beliefs. Her answers seemed weak and submissive. She seemed at a loss for words. Her mind was quick, however, when Wallace asked if birth control, as Catholic leaders claimed, violated natural law. "How do they know?" Sanger replied, "After all, they are celibates, they don't know love, marriage. They know nothing about bringing up children . . . and yet they speak to people as if they were God."[185]

The soft-spoken, strong-willed, silver-tongued pioneer of a vital movement was no longer. Her friends were mortified; her ex-husband, Bill Sanger, cried. Not even Wallace fans liked the interview. Still, she proved once again capable of inspiring public reaction. The opposition sent stacks of letters to her Tucson home. "I pray every day that you may fry in Hell forever,"[186] read one. Sanger quit opening the mail.

Sanger's trip to Tokyo for a four-day conference in October was a glorious celebration for Sanger personally and a grand party for the delegates. The occasion was the Fifth International Conference of the International Planned Parenthood Federation. Sanger was greeted with great honor and respect. In the meantime, Sanger's health continued to decline. She suffered more heart attacks. Her family feared that any additional travel or activities would prove disastrous. Still, in 1959, she insisted on attending the Sixth International Conference on Planned Parenthood in New Delhi, India. She arrived, attended by a Planned Parenthood volunteer, but all the activities overwhelmed the frail Sanger and she left the conference in a wheelchair. But in-between she was applauded and celebrated. The February 14 reception in her honor was a fitting Valentine for the 80-year-old matriarch of birth control. Some 750 delegates from 27 nations applauded as she was escorted before them. The cameras flashed more brightly as she entered because her escort was none other than Prime Minister Nehru. This time he did more than endorse birth control, he pledged $10 million government dollars for family planning. Thrilled, Sanger wrote her granddaughters, "He bent over me and said 'It is wonderful that you come to us from so far away.'"[187] With her sense of history and knowledge of her own place in it, she sent them photographs of the two celebrities together, saying, "Be sure to hold these forever."[188]

The conference was Sanger's last opportunity to reiterate her life's work. She rose to the occasion. Her speech recapped much of what she had been saying all her life. "Overpopulation, poverty, and war could be prevented," she said. "Anyone who has a free mind and the welfare of the nation at heart will recognize that one single principle should stand *first* and *foremost* in solving of these problems, which is birth control."[189]

The next day, Gregory Pincus dedicated his reports on oral contraception to Margaret Sanger. She was too weak to leave her hotel room and celebrated with friends over her favorite lunch—chicken salad sandwiches and champagne.

On February 25, 1959 in Tokyo, Sanger's sixth trip to Japan reaped another important announcement. Japan had cut its birth rate by more than 50 percent in less than a decade, proving that family planning was effective. Her granddaughters, traveling with Sanger on her seventh trip there, were astonished at their grandmother's celebrity.

The United States was nowhere near as accepting of birth control measures. In July 1959, President Dwight D. Eisenhower rejected the recommendations from a study on foreign aid that he had specifically commissioned. The Draper Commission Report had revealed a rise in population in impoverished countries could erase economic gains. It recommended that the United States give funding to countries to help them control their birth rate. Under Catholic pressure, Eisenhower rejected his own committee's recommendation.

The flame in Sanger flared once again. She challenged Eisenhower to a debate to "straighten him out."[190] She scorched the Catholic hierarchy in a letter to the *New York Times*, accusing the Roman Catholic hierarchy of shortsightedness. The letter ran on the front page and prompted more campaign discussion about family planning. One more time, Sanger's name was in newspaper headlines. After the nomination of John F. Kennedy (a Catholic) for president, she threatened to leave the country if he was elected.

Her disdain for Kennedy turned out to be misplaced when, as president, he made it clear that his religion would not be an influence on his decision making. In 1960, Sanger saw several breakthrough events for birth control. President Kennedy resurrected the Draper Report and agreed with its recommendations, saying the United States would help nations that wanted to curb their birth rate. He formed the Sponsors Council for Planned Parenthood-World Federation with two former Presidents, Harry Truman and Dwight Eisenhower, as heads. Eisenhower himself changed his position. "I have come to believe that the population explosion is the world's most critical problem. . . . Governments must act and private citizens must cooperate urgently through voluntary means to secure this right for all peoples,"[191] he wrote. For the first time, it seemed that the government of the United States stood beside Sanger rather than against her.

In another breakthrough event, "the Pill" was released for use in May 1960. The pill was a giant step towards Sanger's goal of bringing a safe and effective form of birth control to the people. Forty years later, 10 million U.S. women take the pill for birth control and more than 50 million have tried it.[192]

In March 1961, the World Population Emergency Campaign organized a tribute to Sanger for her 45 years as a campaigner for birth control. She wrote them, "I cannot tell you how my heart goes out to you for all you are doing. As a matter of fact, you are the only one in recent years who has any knowledge of the history of the Movement or that Margaret Sanger had anything to do with it."[193]

She was wrong. Friends from 35 countries sent congratulations for this "World Tribute to Margaret Sanger." Her steadfast friend Katherine McCormick gave $100,000 for a fund that would carry Sanger's name. Programs for attendees included photos from Sanger's life. Stuart accompanied his fragile mother to New York for the occasion. She gave her thanks to the group and then fell asleep on the podium. She would not awaken and had to be carried to her room. It was her last public appearance.

In 1962, unable to care for herself, Sanger went to a nursing home, and Stuart became her guardian. In the home, she was either bedridden or in a wheelchair. One day she might not seem to recognize visitors and the next day could tell her nurses exactly who they were. She held her great granddaughter, Peggy, for the first time. She thought the baby was her own daughter Peggy who had come back to see her. Her favorite meal remained chicken salad, and she asked nurses to bring her champagne with a straw and cup.

Tucson hailed her as "The Woman of the Century" in a March 1962 testimonial. Stuart represented his mother at the dinner whose guests included the Duke and Duchess of Windsor, representatives of England and India, and presidential candidate (and friend of Sanger's) Barry Goldwater.

On June 7, 1965, the United States Supreme Court, in *Griswold* v. *Connecticut*, struck down state Comstock laws that had made the use of birth control by married couples a crime. The justices found that the law invaded citizens' right to privacy. It had taken half a century for the court to come around to what Margaret Sanger's had been saying all along.

"Birth control is a woman's problem," she wrote in *Woman and the New Race*. "The quicker she accepts it as hers and hers alone, the quicker will society respect motherhood. The quicker, too, will the world be made a fit place for her children to live."[194]

Her affection for Japan was so strong that Sanger once said that her heart should be buried there. Japan cared deeply for her, honoring Sanger with the Third Order of the Sacred Crown. She was only the second person to receive it.

Death and the number 6 merged once more in Sanger's life. On September 6, 1966, Margaret Sanger died in her sleep. The *London Times* and the *New York Times* ran front-page tributes. Ernest Gruen, an Episcopalian minister, eulogized her in the Senate. In the Tucson service, the Episcopal priest told the mourners, "All the elements of sainthood were personified many times in her life."[195]

Some would definitely agree with him; others definitely would not.

On September 21, 1966, the family and birth control colleagues attended a memorial service in New York City, where Sanger would be buried. Margaret Sanger never met any of the presidents who served across her lifeline and was never honored by the country she hoped to improve. But 80-year-old Mrs. Rose Halpern, one of Sanger's first Brownsville Clinic patients, attended the service. In torrential storms, the rector at St. George's described the day as "a stormy day to end a stormy life."[196] No one would argue with that.

Margaret Sanger spoke to groups of hundreds and thousands. She founded organizations that endure, in some form, today. But her life was really directed at helping one woman at a time.

Margaret Sanger refused to believe that women should be treated as second-class citizens. She would not accept governments, laws, or religious organizations reaching into the most private parts of a woman's life and controlling her most important choice—whether or when to conceive a child.

She was arrested, jailed, ridiculed, verbally attacked, spit on, and insulted. But she refused to give up her crusade.

Today, women routinely open a plastic container and absent-mindedly swallow a tiny pill. Others, just as routinely, slap a contraceptive patch on their skin once a week. Still more choose any one of a handful of other birth control methods.

They likely have little idea of the momentous struggle behind these actions. Few, if any, know anything about the tiny red-haired Irish woman who the *New York Times* called "one of history's great rebels and a monumental figure of the first half of the twentieth century."[197] And yet, despite Sanger's contributions, contraception still remains a hot topic. In 2003, controversy focused on the availability of the **morning-after pill**, emergency contraception that is used only after sex. Opponents object to putting it next to condoms on store shelves. Some argue that availability of an over-the-counter morning-after pill will lead to an increase in irresponsible sexual behavior, particularly in young people. Others argue that emergency contraception is in fact a method of early abortion and, as such, should be subject to legislation.

If Margaret Sanger lived today, she would put on her stylish hat, and pick up her purse and white gloves once again. Then she would wade into the debate. She would march into the fray laughing.

She would have heard it all before.

1879   Margaret Louisa Higgins is born in Corning, New York

1895   Margaret attends Claverack College and Hudson
River Institute

1900   Margaret becomes probationary nurse at White Plains
Hospital, New York

1902   Margaret marries Bill Sanger

1903   Margaret Sanger contracts tuberculosis and gives
birth to son Stuart

Timeline

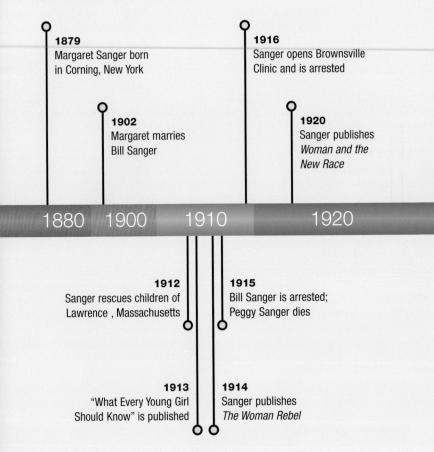

1879
Margaret Sanger born
in Corning, New York

1916
Sanger opens Brownsville
Clinic and is arrested

1902
Margaret marries
Bill Sanger

1920
Sanger publishes
*Woman and the
New Race*

1880   1900   1910   1920

1912
Sanger rescues children of
Lawrence , Massachusetts

1915
Bill Sanger is arrested;
Peggy Sanger dies

1913
"What Every Young Girl
Should Know" is published

1914
Sanger publishes
The Woman Rebel

1908 Sanger's second son, Grant, is born

1910 Daughter Peggy is born; Sanger becomes active
with Socialists

1912 Sanger rescues children of Lawrence, Massachusetts;
she testifies before the House of Representative
Hearings; she meets Sadie Sachs

1913 "What Every Young Girl Should Know" is published
in defiance of the Comstock Act

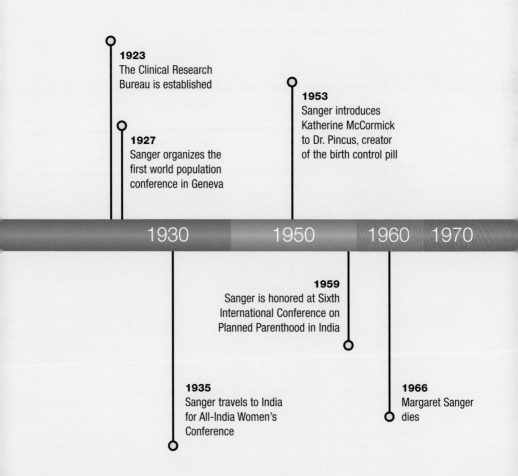

1923
The Clinical Research
Bureau is established

1953
Sanger introduces
Katherine McCormick
to Dr. Pincus, creator
of the birth control pill

1927
Sanger organizes the
first world population
conference in Geneva

1930   1950   1960 1970

1959
Sanger is honored at Sixth
International Conference on
Planned Parenthood in India

1935
Sanger travels to India
for All-India Women's
Conference

1966
Margaret Sanger
dies

Chronology

1914 Sanger publishes *The Woman Rebel;* she coins the term "birth control" and is arraigned for mailing *The Woman Rebel;* Sanger flees to Europe; *Family Limitation* is published

1915 Bill Sanger is arrested; Margaret Sanger visits Holland's birth control clinics; Peggy Sanger dies

1916 Sanger speaks on national tour and opens the Brownsville Clinic; she is arrested again

1917 The Brownsville trial ends; Sanger begins serving 30-day jail sentence; she publishes *The Birth Control Review*

1918 The Crane decision redefines "disease"

1920 Sanger publishes *Woman and the New Race*

1921 Sanger meets J. Noah Slee; her divorce from Bill Sanger is finalized; the American Birth Control League is created; First American Birth Control Conference is held; Sanger is arrested at Town Hall riot

1922 Sanger leaves for Japan and world tour; she marries J. Noah Slee

1923 The Clinical Research Bureau is established

1927 Sanger organizes first world population conference in Geneva

1929 Sanger resigns from the American Birth Control League and *The Birth Control Review;* Sanger is arrested at Clinic Research Bureau raid; the National Committee on Federal Legislation for Birth Control is established

1932 Sanger is honored at American Women's Association Award Dinner

1934 The "doctor's bill" is defeated in the Senate

1935 Sanger travels to India for All-India Women's Conference; she meets Gandhi

1936 One Package decision is announced

1937 Sanger is honored at Town Hall Award dinner

1943 J. Noah Slee dies

1948 International Congress on Population and World Resources is held; International Committee on Planned Parenthood is founded

1949 Sanger receives honorary degree from Smith College; she has her first heart attack

1953 Sanger introduces Katherine McCormick to Gregory Pincus, creator of the birth control pill

1957 Sanger is interviewed by Mike Wallace

1959 Sanger is honored at Sixth International Conference on Planned Parenthood in India

1961 Sanger is honored at "A World Tribute to Margaret Sanger"

1965 Sanger is honored as "Woman of the Century"; she receives Third Class Order of Precious Crown of Japan

1966 Margaret Sanger dies

Glossary

Abortion—The premature termination of a pregnancy.

Anthony Comstock—A self-appointed anti-vice crusader from New York who in the 1870s succeeded in convincing Congress to pass a stringent statute that linked contraception to obscenity.

Birth control—The practice of contraception for the purpose of limiting the number of children born.

Cervical cap—A smaller, more modern version of the diaphragm that is inserted in the vagina and fits over the cervix.

Comstock Law—Law that, among other things, made it a federal offense to disseminate birth control information through the mail or across state lines.

Conception—The fertilization of an egg by a sperm; the act of getting pregnant.

Condom—A thin rubber sheath worn over the penis during intercourse.

Contraceptive—A device, drug, or chemical agent that prevents conception.

Contraception—The intentional prevention of conception or impregnation through the use of various devices, drugs, practices, or surgical procedures.

Diaphragm—A contraceptive device consisting of a flexible dome-shaped cup that fits over the cervix.

Gonorrhea—A common venereal disease caused by the bacterium *Neisseria gonorrhoeae.*

Industrial Workers of the World (IWW)—A radical labor movement that hoped to organize all workers into "one big union" in order to build labor solidarity and defeat capitalism.

Morning-after pill—A large dose of birth control pills that, taken 72 hours after unprotected intercourse, prevents pregnancy.

Oral contraceptives—Birth control pills that generally contain two hormones, an estrogen and a progesterone. They prevent pregnancy by stopping ovulation (release of an egg) and by inhibiting implantation of a fertilized egg.

Ovulation—The release of an egg during a woman's monthly cycle.

Pessary—A rubber ring invented to support a uterus or bladder that had slipped out of position that also was used as a contraceptive.

Progesterone—A steroid hormone produced in the ovary; as a component in the birth control pill, it induces changes in the lining of the uterus that inhibits implantation of a fertilized egg.

Prohibition—The movement that resulted in the 18th Amendment to the Constitution, prohibiting the manufacture, sale or transportation of liquor. It was repealed in 1933.

Racial suicide—The belief that a low birth rate would lead to the extinction of a particular race of people.

Sanatorium—A hospital where people were treated or recuperated from chronic diseases such as tuberculosis.

Socialist Party—A political party that sought to organize society in a way that served for the benefit of all, rather than for the profit of a few.

Spermicide—An agent that kills sperm, usually used with a diaphragm or cervical cap.

Suffrage—The movement to secure voting rights for women; this was accomplished through the 19th amendment to the Constitution.

Syphilis—A venereal disease caused by infection with the microorganism *Treponema pallidum*.

Tubal sterilization—An operation that blocks the tubes carrying a woman's egg to her uterus. Worldwide, it is the most commonly used method of birth control.

Vasectomy—An operation that blocks the tubes (called the vas deferens) that carry a man's sperm to the penis.

Venereal diseases—Communicable diseases transmitted by sexual intercourse.

Notes

Chapter 1

1. Miriam Reed, *Margaret Sanger: Her Life in Her Words* (Fort Lee, N. J.: Barricade Books, 2003), 83.

2. Madeline Gray, *Margaret Sanger: A Biography of the Champion of Birth Control* (New York: Richard Merek Publishers, 1979), 130.

3. Reed, *Margaret Sanger: Her Life in Her Words*, 81.

4. Margaret Sanger, *Margaret Sanger: An Autobiography* (New York: W. W. Norton, 1938), 221.

5. Nancy Whitelaw, *Margaret Sanger: Every Child a Wanted Child* (New York: Dillon Press, 1994), 75.

6. Ellen Chelser, *Woman of Valor: Margaret Sanger and the Birth Control Movement in America* (New York: Simon and Schuster, 1992), 148.

7. Sanger, *An Autobiography*, 214.

8. David M. Kennedy, *Birth Control in America: The Career of Margaret Sanger* (New Haven: Yale University Press, 1970), 85.

9. *New York Times*, September 12, 1916, p. 11.

10. Sanger, *An Autobiography*, 219.

11. Ibid.

12. Chelser, *Woman of Valor*, 151.

13. Gray, *Margaret Sanger: A Biography*, 129.

14. Lawrence Lader and Milton Meltzer, *Margaret Sanger: Pioneer of Birth Control* (New York: Thomas Y. Crowell, 1969), 82.

15. Gray, *Margaret Sanger: A Biography*, 132.

16. Kennedy, *Birth Control in America*, 83.

Chapter 2

17. Sanger, *An Autobiography*, 38.

18. Ibid., 21.

19. Whitelaw, *Margaret Sanger: Every Child a Wanted Child*, 16.

20. Ibid.

21. *Margaret Sanger*, produced by Bruce Alfred, Cobblestone Productions, 1999. Documentary video funded by the National Endowment for the Humanities.

22. Sanger, *An Autobiography*, 38.

23. Ibid., 37.

24. Ibid., 41.

25. Chelser, *Woman of Valor*, 44.

26. Sanger, *An Autobiography*, 42.

27. Kennedy, *Birth Control in America*, 6.

28. Whitelaw, *Margaret Sanger: Every Child a Wanted Child*, 23–24.

29. Ibid.

30. Sanger, *An Autobiography*, 55.

31. Ibid., 56.

32. Chelser, *Woman of Valor*, 48.

33. Whitelaw, *Margaret Sanger: Every Child a Wanted Child*, 25–26.

34. Chelser, *Woman of Valor*, 49.

35. Whitelaw, *Margaret Sanger: Every Child a Wanted Child*, 28.

36. Reed, *Margaret Sanger: Her Life in Her Words*, 12.

37. Chelser, *Woman of Valor*, 54.

38. Sanger, *An Autobiography*, 63.

39. Chelser, *Woman of Valor*, 54.

40. Reed, *Margaret Sanger: Her Life in Her Words*, 12.

Chapter 3

41. Kennedy, *Birth Control in America*, 9.

42. Sanger, *An Autobiography*, 76.

43. Ibid.

44. Chelser, *Woman of Valor*, 62.

45. Kennedy, *Birth Control in America*, 15.

46. Reed, *Margaret Sanger: Her Life in Her Words*, 14.

47. Ibid., 19.

48. Ibid., 21.

49. Ibid., 24.

50. Lader and Meltzer, *Margaret Sanger: Pioneer of Birth Control*, 34.

51. Reed, *Margaret Sanger: Her Life in Her Words*, 29.

52. Sanger, *An Autobiography*, 88–89.

53. Ibid., 91.

54. Ibid.

55. Ibid., 92.

56. Ibid.

57. Reed, p. 32.

58. Chesler, *Woman of Valor*, 66.

59. Reed, *Margaret Sanger: Her Life in Her Words*, 32.

Chapter 4

60. Reed, *Margaret Sanger: Her Life in Her Words*, 35.

61. Whitelaw, *Margaret Sanger: Every Child a Wanted Child*, 42.

62. Chelser, *Woman of Valor*, 81.

63. Reed, *Margaret Sanger: Her Life in Her Words*, 40.

64. Ibid., 41–42.

65. Chelser, *Woman of Valor*, 92.

66. Whitelaw, *Margaret Sanger: Every Child a Wanted Child*, 52.

67. Chelser, *Woman of Valor*, 95.

68. Ibid., 98.

69. Ibid.

70. Reed, *Margaret Sanger: Her Life in Her Words*, 46.

71. Whitelaw, *Margaret Sanger: Every Child a Wanted Child*, 51.

72. Lader and Meltzer, *Margaret Sanger: Pioneer of Birth Control*, 59.

73. Whitelaw, *Margaret Sanger: Every Child a Wanted Child*, 52.

74. Reed, *Margaret Sanger: Her Life in Her Words*, 50.

Chapter 5

75. Lader and Meltzer, *Margaret Sanger: Pioneer of Birth Control*, 60.

76. Whitelaw, *Margaret Sanger: Every Child a Wanted Child*, 54.

77. Chelser, *Woman of Valor*, 105.

78. Ibid.,105.

79. Reed, *Margaret Sanger: Her Life in Her Words*, 57.

80. Sanger, *An Autobiography*, 192.

81. Lader and Meltzer, *Margaret Sanger: Pioneer of Birth Control*, 69.

82. Ibid.

83. Whitelaw, *Margaret Sanger: Every Child a Wanted Child*, 58.

Notes

84. Ibid., 59.

85. Chelser, *Woman of Valor*, 145.

86. Lader and Meltzer, *Margaret Sanger: Pioneer of Birth Control*, 69.

87. Chelser, *Woman of Valor*, 127.

88. Whitelaw, *Margaret Sanger: Every Child a Wanted Child*, 60.

89. *New York Times*, September 12, 1915.

90. Gray, *Margaret Sanger: A Biography*, 112.

91. Lader and Meltzer, *Margaret Sanger: Pioneer of Birth Control*, 75.

92. *New York Times*, January 18, 1916.

93. *New York Times*, February 19, 1916.

94. Gray, *Margaret Sanger: A Biography*, 119.

95. *New York Times*, January 9, 1917.

96. Ibid.

97. *New York Times*, January 23, 1917.

98. *New York Times*, January 25, 1917.

99. *New York Times*, January 26, 1917.

100. Ibid.

101. *New York Times*, January 27, 1917.

102. *New York Times*, January 29, 1917.

103. Gray, *Margaret Sanger: A Biography*, 134.

104. Chelser, *Woman of Valor*, 156.

Chapter 6

105. Gray, *Margaret Sanger: A Biography*, 136.

106. Ibid.

107. *New York Times*, February 6, 1917.

108. Sanger, *An Autobiography*, 237.

109. Whitelaw, *Margaret Sanger: Every Child a Wanted Child*, 90.

110. Gray, *Margaret Sanger: A Biography*, 217.

111. Chelser, *Woman of Valor*, 137.

112. Whitelaw, *Margaret Sanger: Every Child a Wanted Child*, 104.

113. Reed, *Margaret Sanger: Her Life in Her Words*, 129.

114. Lader and Meltzer, *Margaret Sanger: Pioneer of Birth Control*, 101.

115. Sanger, *An Autobiography*, 302.

116. Ibid.

117. *New York Times*, November 14, 1921.

118. Ibid.

119. Reed, *Margaret Sanger: Her Life in Her Words*, 130.

120. *New York Times*, November 15, 1921.

121. Reed, *Margaret Sanger: Her Life in Her Words*, 134.

122. *New York Times*, December 18, 1921.

123. Sanger, *An Autobiography*, 307.

124. Margaret Sanger, *The Pivot of Civilization In Historical Perspective. The Birth Control Classic*, ed. Michael W. Perry (Seattle: Inkling Books, 2001), 168.

125. Sanger, *An Autobiography*, 315.

126. Ibid.

Chapter 7

127. Reed, *Margaret Sanger: Her Life in Her Words*, 234–235.

128. Gray, *Margaret Sanger: A Biography*, 167.

129. Reed, *Margaret Sanger: Her Life in Her Words*, 236.

130. Reed, *Margaret Sanger: Her Life in Her Words*, 141.

131. Reed, *Margaret Sanger: Her Life in Her Words*, 143.

132. Lader and Meltzer, *Margaret Sanger: Pioneer of Birth Control*, 111.

133. Whitelaw, *Margaret Sanger: Every Child a Wanted Child*, 110.

134. Lader and Meltzer, *Margaret Sanger: Pioneer of Birth Control*, 113.

135. Whitelaw, *Margaret Sanger: Every Child a Wanted Child*, 110.

136. Chelser, *Woman of Valor*, 250.

137. Ibid., 259.

138. Ibid., 262.

139. Ibid.

140. Sanger, *An Autobiography*, 394–395.

141. Ibid., 395.

142. Ibid., 403.

143. Ibid.

144. Reed, *Margaret Sanger: Her Life in Her Words*, 178.

Chapter 8

145. Sanger, *An Autobiography*, 409.

146. Chelser, *Woman of Valor*, 327.

147. Reed, *Margaret Sanger: Her Life in Her Words*, 182.

148. Lader and Meltzer, *Margaret Sanger: Pioneer of Birth Control*, 136.

149. Chelser, *Woman of Valor*, 330.

150. Sanger, *An Autobiography*, 420.

151. Ibid., 421.

152. Ibid., 422.

153. Reed, *Margaret Sanger: Her Life in Her Words*, 180.

154. Ibid., 183.

155. Sanger, *An Autobiography*, 425.

156. Gray, *Margaret Sanger: A Biography*, 329.

157. Ibid., 334.

158. Chelser, *Woman of Valor*, 349.

159. Ibid.

160. Ibid., 350.

161. Sanger, *An Autobiography*, 461.

162. Ibid., 471.

163. Ibid., 430.

164. *New York Times*, December 8, 1936.

165. Emily Taft Douglas, *Margaret Sanger: Pioneer of the Future* (New York: Holt, Rinehart and Winston, 1970), 223.

Chapter 9

166. Chelser, *Woman of Valor*, 384.

167. Ibid., 387.

168. Ibid., 387.

169. Gray, *Margaret Sanger: A Biography*, 381.

170. Ibid., 385.

171. Chelser, *Woman of Valor*, 460.

172. Ibid.

173. Ibid., 409.

Notes

174. Reed, *Margaret Sanger: Her Life in Her Words*, 267.

175. Chelser, *Woman of Valor*, 412.

176. Douglas, *Margaret Sanger: Pioneer of the Future*, 248.

177. Chelser, *Woman of Valor*, 413.

178. Gray, *Margaret Sanger: A Biography*, 405.

179. Chelser, 417.

180. Douglas, *Margaret Sanger: Pioneer of the Future*, 255.

181. Reed, *Margaret Sanger: Her Life in Her Words*, 251.

182. Ibid., 251.

Chapter 10

183. *New York Times*, April 15, 1954.

184. Chelser, *Woman of Valor*, 437.

185. *Margaret Sanger*, produced by Bruce Alfred.

186. Gray, *Margaret Sanger: A Biography*, 435.

187. Ibid., 257.

188. Ibid.

189. Sanger, *An Autobiography*, 273.

190. Chelser, *Woman of Valor*, 454.

191. Gray, *Margaret Sanger: A Biography*, 259.

192. Leslie Harris and Lisa Cisneros, "Party for the Pill, Women's Liberation," *Daybreak*, UCSF's electronic daily, June 6, 2000, http://www.ucsf.edu/daybreak/2000/06/06_pillparty.html.

193. Chelser, *Woman of Valor*, 457.

194. Reed, *Margaret Sanger: Her Life in Her Words*, 283.

195. *New York Times*, September 11, 1966.

196. Chelser, *Woman of Valor*, 468.

197. Whitelaw, *Margaret Sanger: Every Child a Wanted Child*, 151.

PRIMARY SOURCES

New York Times, January 18, 1916.

New York Times, February 19, 1916.

New York Times, September 12, 1916. p. 11.

New York Times, January 9, 1917 p. 8.

New York Times, January 23, 1917 p. 20.

New York Times, January 25, 1917, p 20.

New York Times, January 26, 1917, p. 1.

New York Times, January 27, 1917, p. 1.

New York Times, January 29, 1917, p. 4.

New York Times, January 30, 1917 p, 4.

New York Times, February 6, 1917, p. 20.

New York Times, November 15, 1921, p. 1.

New York Times, December 18, 1921 p. 18.

New York Times, April 16, 1954.

Sanger, Margaret. *Happiness in Marriage*. New York: Brentano's, 1926.

Sanger, Margaret. *Margaret Sanger: An Autobiography*. New York: W. W. Norton, 1938.

Sanger, Margaret. *The Pivot of Civilization in Historical Perspective. The Birth Control Classic*, ed. Michael W. Perry. Seattle: Inkling Books, 2001.

SECONDARY SOURCES

Chandrasekhar, S. I. *A Dirty, Filthy Book*. Berkley, CA: University of California Press, 1981.

Chelser, Ellen. *Woman of Valor: Margaret Sanger and the Birth Control Movement in America*. New York: Simon & Schuster, 1992.

Douglas, Emily Taft. *Margaret Sanger: Pioneer of the Future*. New York: Holt, Rinehart and Winston, 1970.

Gray, Madeline. *Margaret Sanger: A Biography of the Champion of Birth Control*. New York: Richard Merek, 1979.

Bibliography

Kennedy, David M. *Birth Control in America: The Career of Margaret Sanger.* New Haven: Yale University Press, 1970.

Lader, Lawrence, and Milton Meltzer. *Margaret Sanger: Pioneer of Birth Control.* New York: Thomas Y. Crowell Company, 1969.

Lunardini, Christine A. *Women's Rights.* Phoenix, AZ: Oryx Press, 1996.

Kennedy, David M. *Birth Control in America: The Career of Margaret Sanger: Pioneer of the Future.* New Haven: Yale University Press, 1970.

Reed, Miriam. *Sanger: Her Life in Her Words.* Fort Lee, NJ: Barricade Books, Inc., 2003.

Whitelaw, Nancy. *Margaret Sanger: Every Child a Wanted Child.* New York: Dillon Press, 1994.

VIDEO
Margaret Sanger, produced by Bruce Alfred, Cobblestone Productions, 1999. Documentary video provided by National Endowment for the Humanities.

WEBSITES
Birth Control in the 1930s. DISCovering U.S. History
http://galenet.gale.com

Cannon, Donald J. The Triangle Shirtwaist Fire
http://www.yale.edu/yup/ENYC/triangle_shirtwaist.html

Cervical Cap
http://www.gynob.emory.edu/familyplanning/cervicalcap.cfm

Diaphragm.
http://www.gynob.emory.edu/familyplanning/diaphragm.cfm

The Facts of Life in a World of Six Billion
http://www.ippf.org/resource/6billion/life.htm

Harris, Leslie and Cisneros, Lisa. Party for the Pill, Women's Liberation
http://www.ucsf.edu/daybreak/2000/06/06_pillparty.html

The 1910s: Era Overview, 1910 - 1919.
Gale Research–DISCovering U.S. History
http://galenet.gale.com/a/acp/netacgi/np.../index

The 1920s: Era Overview, 1920-1929.
Gale Research–DISCovering U.S. History
http://galenet.gale.com

Sanger Opens First Birth Control Clinic, October 16, 1916
http://galenet.gale.com

Supreme Court Forbids Banning of Contraceptives, October, 1964, term
http://galenet.gale.com

Tuberculosis
http://www.lungusa.org/site/pp.asp?c=dvLUK9O0E&b=35778

Further Reading

Basso, Michael J. *The Underground Guide to Teenage Sexuality.* Minneapolis, MN: Fairview Press, 1997.

Connell, Elizabeth B. *Contraception Sourcebook.* Chicago: Contemporary Books, 2002.

Hanson, Erica. *Through the Decades: The 1920s.* San Diego: Lucent Books, 1999.

Peacock, Judith. *Birth Control and Protection Options for Teens.* LifeMatters. Minnesota: Mankato, 2001.

Pietrusza, David. *The Roaring Twenties.* San Diego: Lucent Books, 1998.

Press, Petra. *Through the Decades: The 1930s.* San Diego: Lucent Books, 1999.

Stoppard, Dr. Miriam. *Sex Ed Growing Up, Relationships and Sex.* New York: DK Publishing Inc., 1997.

Uschan, Micael V. *Through the Decades: The 1940s.* San Diego: Lucent Books, 1999.

Winikoff, Beverly and Wymelenberg, Suzanne. *Contraception A Guide to Safe and Effective Choice.* Washington, D.C.: Joseph Henry Press, 1997.

Woog, Adam. *Through the Decades: The 1900s.* San Diego: Lucent Books, 1999.

Index

Index

Index

Picture Credits

page:

29: Sophia Smith Collection, Smith College
30: Sophia Smith Collection, Smith College
31: Sophia Smith Collection, Smith College
32: Sophia Smith Collection, Smith College
33: Sophia Smith Collection, Smith College
34: Sophia Smith Collection, Smith College
35: © Bettmann/CORBIS
36: © Bettmann/CORBIS
37: Sophia Smith Collection, Smith College
38: Reproduced with permission from
    Planned Parenthood® Federation

of America, Inc. © 2004 PPFA. All
rights reserved.
39: © Bettmann/CORBIS
40: © Bettmann/CORBIS
41: Reproduced with permission from
    Planned Parenthood® Federation
    of America, Inc. © 2004 PPFA. All
    rights reserved.
42: Sophia Smith Collection, Smith College
43: © Bettmann/CORBIS

Cover: © Bettmann/CORBIS

About the Author

Vicki Cox is a freelance writer for national magazines and newspapers in sixteen states. In addition to four other Chelsea House biographies, she has authored an anthology of features, *Rising Stars and Ozark Constellations* which profiles people and places on the Ozark Plateau. With an M.S. in Education, she taught public school for twenty-five years, and currently teaches at Drury University in Springfield, Missouri. Her clothes hang in Lebanon, Missouri, but she resides mostly in her car.